PROFESSIONAL -IN- pajamas

101 Tips for Working from Home

Karen Adamedes

Professional in Pajamas: 101 Tips for Working from Home
By Karen Adamedes

Published by:
Abney Hall Pty Ltd
P.O. Box 189
Cremorne, NSW 2090 Australia
info@abneyhall.com

Paperback 2020

ISBN 978 0 9806364 5 1

Other Editions:
ISBN 978 0 9806364 3 7 (EPUB)
ISBN 978 0 9806364 4 4 (MOBI)

Copyright © 2020 by Karen Adamedes
All rights reserved.

This book is copyright. Except for the purposes of fair reviewing no part of this publication may be reproduced or transmitted in any form or by any means, electronic or mechanical, including photocopying, recording or by any information storage and retrieval system, without written permission from the publisher.

This publication is to provide guidance regarding the subject areas covered. However, this is with the understanding that the author and publisher are not providing legal, financial, technical, health or other professional advice.

Preface

I've worked from home for over a decade and have been writing this book for more than a year. That was back in the day when working from home was a choice, a privilege or for many a small business person, a necessity. Now due to COVID-19 it is mandatory for millions as a way of minimizing the spread of the virus and protecting ourselves and others.

We have a new vocabulary that includes self-isolation, physical distancing, lockdown, quarantine and stay-at-home orders. We are all a little bit scared as there are so many things that are out of our control *(I'm sure it's not just me!)* The way we work and live is changing, for now, and we don't know what the new normal will be on the other side of this pandemic.

There are those who are working from home for the first time, who are trying to figure out how to make it work. Like how do you have a professional work conversation when you have children fighting over the remote control in the next room? Or how do you stay connected with colleagues, customers or in fact any other human being if you live alone?

There are others who do work at home regularly or occasionally, who are now confined to their home with no escape to the office for some laughs, giggles or even a boring meeting *(which now has some appeal!)*

And then there are others, like me, who work at home full-time, who are adjusting to working with colleagues and customers who are now working differently *(and calling a lot more often than they used to!)* I have worked at home as both as an employee and as the Principal of my own consultancy business. I love setting my own routine, wearing whatever I feel comfortable in *(as long as I don't have a video conference),* and being able to talk on the phone as loudly as I like.

My office has a huge print that brings color and life to my workspace. I can grab my laptop and work from the garden or in front of the TV, whenever I choose. Sometimes I put on the occasional load of washing during the day, and feel virtuously organized, for a short time at least.

But there are downsides, too. There's the absolute frustration when I have an IT problem, the irritation of the neighbor's lawnmower starting up when I'm on a conference call, and sometimes, a ridiculous and illogical feeling of guilt when I go out for a coffee *(although that is suspended for a while)*. Taking some time out is something I wouldn't think twice about if I worked in an office. And then there is the issue of 'not knowing when to call it quits and stop working' because I can always find something else to do.

Through trial and error, and comparing notes with others who work from home, I found that there *are* ways to manage the drawbacks. The more people I talked to – from different countries and industries, occasional or full-time work-at-homers, employees or those who work for themselves – the more I found that many of us struggle with the same challenges.

This started me on a quest to figure out how to make working from home really work. With not a lot of ways to easily connect with other people who work from home I decided this book would be the ideal way to share what I have learnt.

Thank you to my many friends and colleagues who generously gave their time to tell me about their experiences, and were good humored enough to share their stories about what *really* happens when you work from home.

I have not rewritten the book to reflect what is going on today but I think it is all relevant. Except a couple of tips like leaving the house once a day, interacting with human beings in person and going to the office sometimes – you might need to put these on hold for now if you are in self-isolation, lockdown, quarantine or whatever. In our current crazy world I really hope that it will provide you with some ideas and insights that will help make working from home, work for you.

We are in this together. By working from home we are doing our little bit to help beat this thing.

Stay safe.

Karen Adamedes

Contents

Preface..iii

WORKING FROM HOME xi

    The good stuff (why we love it)...xv

    What could possibly go wrong? (what we need to manage) xix

I.   GETTING STUFF DONE *(how to be productive)* 1

    1. Know what you want to achieve...2

    2. Schedule your time 4

    3. Have a shower...7

    4. Work during your most productive part of the day 8

    5. Play music (sometimes) 11

    6. Restrict home/work multi-tasking 12

    7. Avoid distractions 14

    8. Include something you enjoy in every day 16

    9. Manage time with friends...18

    10. Put your phone on silent 19

    11. Turn off email notifications..20

    12. Limit social media..22

    13. Use an out-of-office email response 23

    14. Pick up the phone...25

    15. Find a routine 27

	16. Take breaks 29
	17. Build a virtual team..31
	18. Focus on success 33
	19. Make time to work...35
II.	WORK VERSUS HOME *(how to keep the balance)* 37
	20. Dedicated office space 38
	21. Agree boundaries with your household 40
	22. Create your own commute 42
	23. Outsource 45
	24. Signal your availability..47
	25. Limit personal intrusions 49
	26. Agree the plan 50
	27. Leave your device in your office 52
	28. Pack up for the weekend 54
	29. Let people know when you're done for the day 55
	30. Train your colleagues..56
	31. Develop strategies to combine work and home 58
III.	WHERE YOU WORK *(how to be comfy)*...............................61
	32. Lighting..62
	33. Temperature 65
	34. Chair...66

	35.	Setting up your workstation 67
	36.	Stock up on office supplies 70
	37.	Shred it!..72
	38.	Lockable storage 73
	39.	Insurance 74
	40.	Create your space 75
	41.	Bits and pieces 77
IV.	TECHNOLOGY *(how to geek)* 79
	42.	Fast connectivity 80
	43.	Plan B for IT 81
	44.	Store documents in the cloud..83
	45.	Backup your work...85
	46.	Video conferencing 86
	47.	Two screens...89
	48.	Security software 91
	49.	System updates..93
	50.	Tech support..94
V.	CONFERENCING *(how to maximize your impact)* 95
	51.	Prepare your background (for video calls)..........................97
	52.	Minimize background noise..98
	53.	Close the door 100

54. Disclose your plans 101

55. Prepare to share (your screen) 102

56. Test the technology 104

57. Dress appropriately 105

58. Get yourself ready 107

59. Switch to silent 109

60. Use your mute button 110

61. Sit up straight 111

62. Introduce yourself 113

63. Have something to say 114

VI. KEEP IN TOUCH *(how to stay top of mind)* 115

64. Be available 116

65. Check in 118

66. Use video 119

67. Stay in contact with your manager/client 120

68. Take time to build rapport 123

69. Call 126

70. Go to the office (sometimes) 127

71. Share your wins 128

72. Connect 130

73. Get involved in activities 132

VII.	CAREER DEVELOPMENT *(how to choose your future)* 135
	74. Set goals 137
	75. Have a plan 140
	76. Get a mentor...142
	77. Identify sponsors and influencers..........................146
	78. Invest in learning..147
	79. Network..149
	80. Follow up after a networking event 151
	81. Be professionally active online.............................153
	82. Recognize when it is time to move on..................154
VIII.	WELL-BEING *(how to look after you)* 157
	83. Move it (that means you!)....................................158
	84. Leave the house once a day 161
	85. Schedule exercise...163
	86. Remember to eat 164
	87. Lunch away from your desk 166
	88. Manage your hours 168
	89. Interact with human beings (in person) 171
	90. Plan meals in advance..173
	91. Change your environment....................................175
	92. Sick? Take the day off..177

CONTENTS ix

93.	Pay yourself back time	178
94.	Claim expenses	180
95.	Drink water	181
96.	Have healthy snacks on hand	183
97.	Buy a fish	185
98.	Take vacations	187
99.	Enjoy the flexibility	189

AND FINALLY, ... 191

100.	Own it!	191
101.	The pajamas dilemma	193

Stay in Touch 195

About the Author 196

Endnotes 197

WORKING FROM HOME

Sandy arrived home from her early morning run with a comfortable 10 minutes to spare before her first call on a Monday. Hair up, face glistening from the exertion of accelerating up the final hill as she made her way home, comfortable in her activewear, Sandy was ready for the day ahead. Until, that is, she realized her first meeting of the day was a video call… and it was due to start in 10 minutes! Panic set in. Until she realized she only needed to worry about what would be seen on the screen.

A quick change of shirt and a bit of subtle lighting, and Sandy was good to go. She made it through the meeting then wandered down to the local coffee shop to make some more calls *(definitely not video ones!)*. Sandy's experience kind of sums up what working at home can be like: great flexibility, but a few drawbacks that are a little bit different to those of our office-based colleagues.

If you've ever worked from home you'll no doubt have a story or two about the ups and downs of working this way. The perils and inconvenience of video conferences, badly behaved pets and long hours seem to feature heavily in the stories I hear – as are the joys of not having to commute, and the flexibility and freedom to manage your own time. Figuring out how to make the most of the positives of working from home and minimizing the pitfalls is the challenge for many of us. Because working from home is a thing. A very big thing.

It's not just you

Working from home has become an accepted way for many of us to work. It's no longer a synonym for a 'day off', seen as a 'perk', or subject to cynicism about how productive people can actually be at home *(well not too often anyway… there are still some doubters out there)*. Working from home, remote working, telecommuting, flexible working – whatever you want to call it – is now a very common way of working for many people.

And it is, for many, many people. A 2017 survey[i] released by Gallup reported that 43% of employed Americans said they spent at least some time working from home. It's not quite as big in some other countries but it's still significant. In Australia, the Australian Bureau of Statistics[ii] released figures in 2016 that showed that almost a third (3.5 million) of all employed persons regularly worked from home in their main job or business. In the UK, the number was 4.2 million in the first three months of 2014[iii], amounting to 13.9% of the workforce. The numbers for Canada are a little older, but in 2008 there were 1.7 million paid employees[iv] (excluding self-employed people!) who worked at home at least one day a week.

That's a lot of people who work from home in just these four countries. *(Technically I know the United Kingdom is not a country…but work with me here.)* My point is that working from home is now very commonplace and there are a lot of us doing it! *(Update: it's now almost everyone!)*

There has been a lot of discussion about the relative productivity of employees who work from home versus those in an office, and the benefits for both employees and employers. In fact, I just searched 'benefits of work from home for employers' and there were 201 million results. And 'benefits of work from home for employees' yielded more than twice as many with 419 million results *(I'll leave those for you to look through!)*

The ability to work from home is often cited as a desirable employment condition and important to ensure diversity in the workforce. This includes the ability of parents with young children, children looking after aging parents, carers, and people with disabilities, as well as those living in regional or remote areas to participate in the workforce. It also provides employers with access to a greater pool of people with valuable skills and expertise.

Discussions are often from the perspective of employers. However, there is not much information available for those of us who work from home about how to make it work better for us. That's what this book is about: embracing the positive aspects and minimizing the potential downsides.

Let's talk about what it's really like

If you are reading this book there is a very good chance you are part of the horde of workers whose morning commute is from the bedroom to the computer *(with a quick detour via the coffee machine),* or you are at least contemplating working from home. *(Update: or have no choice due to the coronavirus.)*

You might work for an organization, manage a portfolio career, freelance, or be a small business owner who sets up shop at the kitchen table at night to manage the paperwork associated with running a business, such as invoices, customer quotes and managing an inbox full of endless emails.

Working from home can be a full-time gig, a couple of days a week or, for some people, just every now and then. Working at home on a Friday seems to be growing in popularity for employees as a chance to catch-up on the work that doesn't get done when you are running from meeting to meeting in the office during the week. Many small business owners or consultants spend Sunday afternoon *(and night!)* preparing for the week ahead.

Regardless of the type of job you have, if you work for an organization or yourself, or how often you are working from home – you want it to work for you. When it does, it's fantastic. Flexibility, no travel time or traffic to deal with, and no noisy colleague in the cubicle next-door are just some of the many benefits of this gig.

But it doesn't always go to plan, and there are some frustrations that need to be dealt with. Unlike in the office there is no colleague at the next desk or in the office kitchen to chat with and mull over your business issues. It's just you! *(And maybe Fido or Kitty – they might be cute but unlikely to be much help.)*

Being someone who works from home is kind of like being a member of a secret society. You are on your own much of the time. You don't know who else is a member. You have a lot in common with people you don't know because you're working in the same way. It can be really helpful to understand the challenges that other members are dealing with and learn about the clever ideas they have come up with to take advantage of the best aspects and deal with the not-so-good ones of working from home.

A shared understanding

When you come across someone who also works from home, it's great to talk to someone who understands your working environment. Not too long ago, I was on an early-morning phone call with a colleague who also works from home. I mentioned that I had a video conference that day. *"Aargh,"* she replied with a combined grin and grimace in her voice, as she knew full well the time it would take me to prepare: hair, make up, business clothes, as well as checking my camera angles and office setup.

"No big deal" office workers would say. They are used to running around the house getting themselves *(and others)* organized, and then battling the morning commute to get to their office. Working from home is just… different. A work-from-home buddy understands that the time taken to prepare for a video conference is a temporary loss of one of the benefits. You can't wait until 6pm for your morning shower *(yes I am guilty of this!)* if you have to look presentable for a video conference earlier in the day.

There is no water cooler to hang around to share ideas with colleagues, pick up tips from others, or just enjoy some chitchat or lively banter. But voilà… in my book, *Professional in Pajamas: 101 Tips for Working from Home*, we can have a chat about how to make working from home, work for us.

When researching this book, everyone I talked to was very generous in sharing their time and ideas about their work-from-home experience. I feel like there is a real drive for us to help each other.

So let's have a chat about the good, the bad and the ugly of working from home and the 101 tips to make it work for you.

The good stuff (why we love it)

No frustrating crawl in the traffic on the freeway. No battling in the rain at the bus stop with an umbrella that has blown inside out from a gust of wind. No smelly commuters packed into a train like a tin of sardines to contend with. None of that for the work-from-home brigade! *(Update: or pretty much anyone at the moment!)*

Best of all, we save approximately an hour a day in travel time compared to those who trek to an office every day. The worldwide average commute is said to be around 41 minutes[v] each way. That's a lot of time standing squished up with strangers, or sitting bumper to bumper in rush-hour traffic.

No wonder the time and aggravation saved on travel is often cited as one of the top benefits of working from home. In a survey I conducted about working from home, a London-based writer told me: *"Cutting out my commute time means I can start my workday earlier and get on top of all my work."* And an Australian IT worker I interviewed said that he spends the time saved on commuting with his family. Another perspective came from someone working in digital PR in the UK who said that they sleep a little later on the days they work from home, take the morning a little easier, and tackle the tasks of the day with a clear mind. Last year, on Twitter @haleymbryant claimed that she had already saved 360 hours commuting by September of that year. Although she did admit that she had used the extra hours from January through to March for napping! However you use the time, it's yours to take back, and you get to choose how to use it.

But wait there's more

Other people said what they like about working from home is the ability to focus without constant interruptions. David Stone, who is encouraged by his company in Australia to work from home a couple of days a week, enjoys being able to focus on key tasks without distractions – and hanging out the washing while he is on a conference call! For Marissa, an Account Manager, working from home means that she doesn't have to worry about disturbing her colleagues: *"I can move about freely up and down my hallway or kitchen (you name it) when speaking with customers on the phone as loud as I want and not worry about disturbing anyone."*

Other work-from-homers said they like that they don't need to watch the clock to make sure they beat the traffic or catch the train at the end of the day. Not needing to worry about personal safety if leaving work late is also seen as a plus. *(Unless you leave the lights off... the 30-second walk from the study to the kitchen, while not great for your daily step tally, isn't usually too dangerous.)*

The ability to make beds in the morning or do dull household chores throughout the day *(put a load of washing on here, unpack the dishwasher there)* can help with the constant work–life balance challenge. Being home for deliveries, spending more time with your kids/ partner/ friends/ dog *(or all of them!),* and the peace and quiet to think, plan and actually do our work... these are just some of the other reasons why working from home is so good.

Freedom and flexibility

A common theme is the freedom and flexibility to manage our day. It allows us *(within the constraints of what we need to do)* to work at times that suit our lifestyle or allow us to maximize our productivity or creativity. It can offer the flexibility to live where we choose. It can provide opportunities to go for a walk in the middle of the day *(weather permitting)*, take a break to pick up the kids from school, buy food for dinner or actually make it to a gym class on time.

I often go for a walk in the morning, have a coffee, then get straight into the day with a break a couple of hours later for a shower *(and, truth be told, another coffee)* when I need to recharge. At the risk of sharing too much information, I often do my best thinking in the shower as I let my thoughts wander. Much better than when I am sitting in front of a computer watching the number of unread emails in my inbox growing like a beanstalk that even Jack couldn't climb. I don't find that encourages my creativity or the ability to solve problems. Funnily enough mid-morning showers are not an option on the days when I am in an office, so I try and take full advantage of how I work best when I'm at home.

It's the flexibility that I, and many other work-from-homers, absolutely love. In a LinkedIn post about working from home Adjunct Professor Kate Skinner-Luker wrote, *"My life and time are finally my own, my work quality and quantity has vastly improved and... I don't. feel. lonely. at all."*

Productivity soars

Like Kate, many people (*including me*), believe that they are much more productive at home. In the same LinkedIn discussion, Author and Coach Donald J ("DJ") Sebastian said, *"I estimate that I was 3 times more productive by working remote than if I camped out in a company office."* Director of Account Management Operations, Rick Glass commented, *"I feel WAY more productive and accomplished working remotely."*

There are numerous studies from recognized institutions such as Stanford University and Harvard Business School that support the fact that people who work remotely are more productive and more engaged, and that this way of working reduces attrition, sick days and facilities costs for employers *(do a quick search to find plenty of supporting statistics if you have a manager that still needs to be convinced!)*.

If you're working, it's better to spend your time on what you need to do rather than commuting, chatting or being dragged into endless meetings. For many of us that means working in our own environment.

Choose where to work

There's also the ability to work in a location that you like. Posts on social media are filled with hashtags, including #workfromhome, #workfromanywhere, #remoteworking, and they show pictures of the views people have while they are working; beaches, gardens, swimming pools and mountain vistas all feature quite heavily. Not to mention the number of snaps of laptops in coffee shops posted by workers who are clearly quite happy not to be stuck in the confines of an office. *(Update: I am sure this will resume at the other side of the virus!)*

Your local coffee haunt, a park, a garden... anywhere with Wi-Fi can become your office for a day or even a short time to provide a change of scenery. And if there isn't Wi-Fi you can always take your own! Mobile Wi-Fi and smart-phone hot spots are liberating. Work from anywhere is the new work from home. Ducking out of the office (even when it's your home that you choose to work in) for a break or new environment is all part of the freedom and flexibility.

It's personal

While there are many good things in common for those of us who work from home it's not the same for everyone. There are a multitude of other benefits including reduced childcare costs and hassles, the ability to live and work where you want, flexibility with your availability and many, many more.

What could possibly go wrong? (what we need to manage)

A laptop, a phone and internet access. What more is there to working from home? What could possibly go wrong? Unfortunately, working from home is not all endless coffee breaks, parcel deliveries, and being able to produce amazing work. Sometimes it can be tough. So let's have a quick chat about the bad and the, sometimes, ugly downside, that is the trade-off for all of the good reasons to work from home. The things that can go wrong. Very wrong.

Author Louisa de Lange *(aka @paperclipgirl)* tweeted a little while back that working at home has some advantages, but added, *"These guys aren't one of them. Peaceful it ain't..."* The accompanying picture? A tree surgeon vehicle unloading what looked like some pretty noisy tree-removal equipment. I know from personal experience that writers don't need too much excuse to stop working and look out the window *(practically nothing in my case)*, but neighborhood background noise can be extremely annoying and frustrating when you are working from home.

Annoying or intrusive noises interrupt your concentration and are distracting when you are on a call. But it's manageable and unlikely to be the biggest hurdle you'll need to overcome when you work from home. The truth is it can be a little bit lonely, the hours can be long, and it can be really tricky to manage those parts of your life where work and home converge.

Research supports that some things suck

Research supports that there are downsides to working away from an office. A 2017 report by Eurofound[vi] (the European Foundation for the Improvement of Living and Working Conditions) found that the biggest drawbacks of what they refer to as telework/ICT mobile work are *"the tendency to lead to longer working hours, to create an overlap between paid work and personal life (work–home interference), and to result in work intensification."*

I agree. And I suspect I am not the only one. Jo MacDonald, owner of a global Executive Search business based in London, admits she sometimes finds it hard to switch off when she works from home because there is always something she could be doing.

Other studies found that when people have more autonomy over their hours, they work longer[vii], and that there are unintended consequences of work intensification[viii] as a result of flexible work practices. It's not all fun and games, coffee breaks, and chats on the phone.

It's work. It can be hard work and it can be lonely. A study, led by a Stanford Economics Professor Nicholas Bloom, of workers from a Chinese company who volunteered to work from home for the duration of the study[ix] found that the workers were happier and more productive at home. However after the nine-month study concluded, half of the participants returned to work. Why? They felt isolated and were concerned that it was bad for their career *(and potential bonus payments!)*.

Not to mention…

Like the study volunteers, people often worry about the impact on their career trajectory. They may also be concerned that others think they're not taking their career or work seriously, or that their colleagues are resentful of the 'perk' they have *(even if it's just the ability to get out of endless meetings)*. And there are some managers who still think you need to be working in an office to be seen to be working *(maybe they are a little envious too… just saying!)*

Then there are the perils associated with managing your own technology and the dangers of conference calls. You are no doubt familiar with 'BBC Dad' who, while being interviewed by the BBC, had his two children followed by his wife enter the room. But did you hear the one about the government official in Pakistan who appeared with the cat-filter turned on during a press conference that was being live streamed on social media? Yep, you read that right. Cat-filter: ears and whiskers superimposed on the official's face *(and two of his colleagues!)*. It resulted in some official government explanations – and some pretty hilarious tweets. An auto-filter and human error were blamed for the mishap. All sorts of technology mishaps can occur when you work from home and there's no on-site IT department to help you out or call on in an emergency.

Some people get distracted, others get so involved in their work they forget to eat, and then there are those who declare their fridge to be a major temptation. Young children, teenagers who commando crawl across the room while you are presenting on a video conference because they desperately need something *(true story, not mine and I am sure my amazing goddaughter will recognize herself in this story)*, loud knocks on the door, family members or housemates that think you should be available 24/7, and barking pooches; there is plenty of potential for things that you can't control to go wrong when your home is also your office.

Is it worth it?

The decision about whether working from home is right for you, comes down to whether the good things outweigh the annoying and frustrating stuff. It's not for everybody. I have two friends named Steven. Steven McDonald never works from home because he gets easily distracted. He says he would stop work to iron, clean, shop, watch TV, or any other diversion that he could find. Steven Ahn didn't work from home for many years because of the stigma of slacking off. But when he worked for a company where it was legitimately accepted as a way of working, he embraced the ability to be able to put on a load of washing between calls and manage his own time.

It's different for everyone. It really is an individual decision. The good news is that there are ways to mitigate the pitfalls and manage the downside so that you can make the most of all the good stuff. Here are 101 tips for you to consider…

I. GETTING STUFF DONE *(how to be productive)*

It can be difficult to compare the productivity of those who work from home to that of office-bound colleagues and clients. It's a little easier if you work at home just a couple of days a week, or even less frequently, as the benchmark is how effective you are compared to days when you are in the office. *"I get so much more done when I work from home"* is often the refrain from people who do both. This is usually followed by a lament that they can't work from home more often.

No matter how frequently you work from home, the purpose is to get stuff done. In work time. Not yours. Quality work, produced in an efficient manner, making good use of your valuable time. This is our goal.

However there are distractions, frequent opportunities to procrastinate and inefficient work practices *(how many browsers do you have open at the same time?)* that can impact our effectiveness when working from home *(or is that just me?)*.

David Morris, an experienced Client Relations Manager and Sales Coach, has worked from home a day a week for many years. He says he definitely gets more done on his work-at-home day. He uses a list of 'to dos' each day to stay on track, so he's not tempted to go out for coffee or lunch, or even mow the lawn. *(I can assure you I have never once been tempted to mow the lawn.)* David says this technique helps to manage the distractions so that he can achieve his goals on his precious work-from-home days.

Some simple processes, tools and approaches to work can make all the difference in the battle against wasting your day *(or having other people hijack it)*. Scheduling your time, finding a routine that works for you, and working during your most productive part of the day can all help make the most of your time. While knowing what you want to achieve and focussing on success will ensure that you are working on the right things.

Combine these with some productivity hacks – like turning off your email notifications, putting your phone on silent, and limiting social media – and you start to build a set of practices to work efficiently.

Let's have a chat about some of the ways to get stuff done.

1. Know what you want to achieve

It really doesn't matter if you work from home or at an office – if you don't know what you want to achieve in a day, you're not going to know if you've had a successful day or not.

Working from home can be a lot less structured than an office environment, and there isn't anyone else but you to set the pace of the day. No one else will know if you are working on what's most important.

When you're on a deadline for a client or a project, it's potentially stressful but can certainly make you focused and clear about what you have to achieve. However, there can be many days when you have the flexibility to choose what you want to work on. Unless you particularly enjoy working in a last-minute panic, prioritizing your time will help ensure you are working on the right things, first.

Knowing what you want to achieve in a day or even a week will help you determine the priorities for the day. If you make a not-so-quick check of social media here, cruise around a couple of news sites, order some shoes online *(oh wait, that might be just me)*, and reply to a couple of text messages, you can find that hours have mysteriously vanished.

Duncan Young, Head of Workplace Health & Well-being at Lendlease in Australia, says, *"Small positive steps can make a big difference over time. Be intentional with your time."* Duncan recommends spending some time each morning planning.

A plan will help you work out what you have to get done, what you'd like to work on, and the 'wouldn't it be amazing if I could do this too' priorities for the day. When you know what your goals are, and how much you have to do, it can help you refocus after interruptions and drag yourself back to your most important tasks after other distractions *(phone calls, emails, and meetings that you can't avoid)*.

This may fall in to the Too Much Information category, but I find having my morning shower is a good time to decide what my top priorities are for the day. For others, taking a morning walk or getting dressed for the day are equally good activities to think through the day ahead. Whatever works for you!

I've also found that writing a 'Top Priorities' list before I finish work for the day can set me up well for the following day. What I have to get done is fresh in my mind, and if I write a list *(or sometimes just sticky notes attached to the bottom of my computer screen),* I know I am not going to forget anything important. This also helps me separate from work at the end of the day, and I don't spend the evening thinking *(quite so much)* about the next day. I have a clear plan of what I need to be focused on when I start work the next morning.

One tip from the Chief Operating Officer of a start-up, who gets constantly interrupted when at the office, is to make sure that on the days you work from home, you have specific tasks to complete or conference calls scheduled. This helps, they said, to take advantage of the quiet and avoid the distractions of being at home.

Working from home is not a full-time gig for everyone. You may only work from home on the days that you need some peace and quiet away from the office or to fit in with personal commitments.

No matter how often you work from home, it pays to focus on the outcomes for the day. You will better prioritize your time, it helps you to avoid distractions, and at the end of the day you will know you have been successful. You can quit for the day feeling satisfied, pat yourself on the back, and know that you achieved what you wanted.

2. Schedule your time

Planning your day is not, by any means, a revolutionary concept. And there is absolutely no shortage of tools to help you schedule your meetings, calls and work time. Calendars, apps, or a good old pen and paper will all do the trick. It doesn't really matter which one you use – as long as you use one.

If you work for a company or organization it makes sense to use whatever they use. If you run your own business or are a part of the gig economy, choose what works best for your clients and you.

The ingenuity in scheduling isn't just in doing it *(let's consider this a brush your teeth in the morning / you should be doing it anyway activity)*. It's about making sure you include sufficient time in your day to get done what you want to do and what needs to be done. There is no point in working from sun up to sun down and the day just disappearing. It's frustrating and disappointing when you don't have any sense of achievement at the end of the day or have to work longer and longer hours.

There are certainly distractions when you work in an office, but at home, unless the phone rings, there are fewer cues to log off social media, stop unpacking the dishwasher or play with the cat to get back to work.

It can also work the other way and you just power from one call to another, back to email, and then on to something else. This is exhausting and means you are always in 'doing' mode with no break or time to think. This can impact your creativity and the quality of what you produce. And it kind of defeats the purpose of working from home.

Here are a few tips for *how* to schedule your time:

Know what time you are going to start and finish your workday

A start time will help you avoid procrastination in the morning *(me: just one more coffee before the computer goes on...)*, and a planned finish time will assist you to stay on track.

Allocate time to take breaks

We talk about this more in the Well-being section of this book, and the reasons for this are many. But they won't happen if they aren't in your schedule. Book them in!

Leave a 15-minute break between meetings

This will give you time to grab a water, visit the bathroom, take a breath, and start thinking about the next topic. Being properly prepared for the next meeting will make you more efficient. And you'll never be late, as you'll always have extra time as the day goes on and other meetings go over time.

Schedule enough time to get 'in the zone'

When you have something important to work on, you need to have enough time to get stuck into it and get a good chunk of it done without interruptions. It takes time to shift gears between activities, think about what you are doing, and get into a real rhythm.

I love writing presentations *(I know… nerd alert!)* I need time to think. What do I want to achieve? How am I going to set it out? What's the flow of the story? Do I need more data? Is there a better word I could use to explain something? What else do I want to say? These are just some of the thought processes I go through. It takes uninterrupted time to get in the zone and produce quality work. I can't pick it up and put it down in half-hour chunks. I need enough time to make some progress. The end result is better and I'm happier. Win – win.

Allocate email time

Whether you like it or not you know those emails are just going to keep coming. They are going to take time each day. Setting aside a couple of email time slots in your calendar will mean that responding to emails doesn't eat into time for other activities and you can keep on track.

The reality is you probably need three time slots a day: morning *(to check what's been sent overnight or first thing)*; middle of the day *(to keep on top of the inbox)*; and afternoon *(to ensure you are responding in a timely manner... and to log off with peace of mind that there is nothing urgent that you haven't dealt with).*

It can be a bit scary when you allocate the time to see how much of your day email consumes. But it is a key way to communicate – with your manager, colleagues, customers or clients and it is important to stay in touch. The good news is that if you don't use all the time you allocate that's a bonus!

Schedule time to plan your day

First thing in the morning, just before you quit for the day or any other time – you will need time to schedule your day or plan out your week. Don't forget to include this activity in your schedule!

3. Have a shower

It can be very tempting to stumble out of bed, turn on the laptop for a quick check of your email, but then find that one email leads to another, you remember something else you needed to do, and before you know it hours *(and hours)* have gone by.

Getting ready for the day can help get you into 'work mode' and approach work more productively. It doesn't mean you need to be sitting at your desk in a suit. The feedback I've had from people who work from home is that the process of getting ready for the day helps them to focus on work. It doesn't actually have to be taking a shower. It could be a bath. The point is to have a routine for preparing for work.

First thing in the morning is a great time to get in some exercise for the day before starting work. Rather than pajamas, you may find yourself still in your activewear as the hours tick by. This can be super comfortable for a while, but time-out for a shower will give you a break, some thinking time about your next priority, and help set you up to be productive. Work for an hour or so when you are fresh from your exercise, but then take a break to transition to the next part of your day.

So pajamas, activewear... wetsuit? Not so comfortable, even if you're a mad keen surfer like Sales Director Richard Webbe, who has worked in the IT industry from home in both the UK and Australia. He says it's wonderful to start the day with a surf, but he has found himself still wearing his wetsuit hours later when calls and emails thwarted his attempts to transition from the waves to the desk. Clammy, constricting, and just a little bit uncomfortable... working in a wet suit made for a funny story but not a great start to a productive working day.

Be comfortable, feel fresh and be ready to take on the day. You'll be more productive, feel better and won't have to hide if there's a knock on the door *(and you won't smell either!)*.

4. Work during your most productive part of the day

Fabian Venter, a marketing consultant based out of the Bay Area in California, takes full advantage of working from home. He starts super early in the morning when he is fresh and feeling creative. Often this is at 5am and he finishes up in the early afternoon. *(If I started that early, I'd be finished by breakfast time, I reckon!).*

I used to work with Fabian, and by the time I got to the office and suggested a first cup of coffee he was already halfway through his day and talking about how beautiful the sunrise had been that morning. I was happy to take his word for it. Fabian had done more than half of what he needed for the day before I even got into the swing of things. Fortunately, we had some part of the working day that crossed over and were able to work well together when we were both feeling productive.

Early bird or Night owl?

There is a lot of advice around about getting started early in the day and the morning being the best time to be productive. The reality, however, is that this is not the case for everyone and just not possible for some. If you have children to drop at school or childcare, or you really want to do your exercise in the morning or a host of other reasons – it can mean that a later start suits you better. Working work around your lifestyle is one of the great benefits of working from home.

Night owls can take advantage of the discretion they have for organizing their day. This means they can get stuck into something important at the time that works for them, when the phones have stopped ringing and colleagues and clients have stopped working *(or at least gone quiet on email)* for the day. Early birds can churn out a presentation while they watch the sunrise. Or you could be a productive fiend in the middle of the day. There is a good chance you know when you are most productive. If not, pay attention to the rhythms of your working day and see if a pattern emerges.

Despite the general consensus that we all have a post-lunch slump, it's not the same for everyone. Research[i] shows that people have 90 to 120 minute cycles, which result in unproductive troughs and then go back to productive peaks. Circadian rhythms (basically your body clock) mean that despite your desire to power through all day, every day – there are times when you are much more productive than others.

Author Pamela Freeman, who also writes as Pamela Hart, has worked from home since 1989. Pamela says working from home is just a habit for her now and suggests that you *"Respect your circadian rhythms."* She says she does her best work in the afternoon.

While researching this book I found that a number of times are suggested as being the most productive: from 9am–11am, from 11am–1pm, and 4–6pm. While it is recognized that this is different for different people, there does seem to be a fair bit of agreement that 1–3pm is a bit of a dead zone… due to our body clocks, rather than eating too much lunch.

Scheduling important work for the times of day that you are most productive is integral to doing your best work. And it lets you schedule your breaks, regular meetings or other activities in the times when you hit a bit of a slump.

I have been reorganizing my days, allocating the tasks where I really need to concentrate to my highly productive times, and making phone calls and emails in the early afternoon. Based on my sample of one *(me)*, it has been making a difference and I'd suggest you give it a go.

It's not just about you

Sad but true. You might be working from home, but you still need to work with other people. Your interactions and communications with others will determine your effectiveness and your reputation – the perception of how capable you are and how easy you are to work with. Which means that you need to talk with them at mutually convenient times, not just when it suits you.

This might mean that you can't always reserve the best part of your day for what you want to do. But you can certainly try. If others schedule meetings at a time that you need to be working on a task, just ask if another time suits. The worst they can say is no, and the best outcome is you will get your precious productive time back. You'll never know if you don't ask.

Work on what is most important during the most productive time of your day, and you'll be delighted by what you achieve *(and you may not need to work as long – bonus!)*.

5. Play music (sometimes)

Music before, during or after work can be a wonderful thing. It can be energizing, soothing, inspirational, or just plain enjoyable.

Career Coach Heather Coleman-Voss has her own business based in the Midwestern US state of Michigan. Heather says playing music is one of the things she loves about working from home as it helps her get excited about everything she will accomplish that day.

Science backs up that she is on the right track. Cognitive neuroscientist Daniel Levitin advises to listen to music for 10–15 minutes[ii] before you start work as a way to boost your productivity.

Overall creativity, efficiency and general happiness are some of the benefits[iii] of listening to music. The downside for music lovers is that the research suggests that only certain music (classical and instrumental) is helpful while you work, as songs with lyrics can be quite distracting. It can depend on what kind of activity you are doing, whether you're writing something new or doing a repetitive task. Experiment and find out what works for you.

One of the added bonuses of working from home is that you don't have to listen to the music your co-worker has chosen. And you can have complete silence when you want to concentrate. You aren't confined to playing your music only through headphones. If you are home alone you can go for it and even have a sing-along!

If you travel for work and spend any time in trains, planes or other forms of transportation, this can be an ideal time to play your music or catch-up on podcasts. Headphones are necessary in these circumstances *(sadly, there's probably no singing along either.)*

Whether you play music to pump you up before you start work, stimulate your creativity, or signal a break or the end of your working day – if, when and what you play when you work from home is up to you. Just one of the reasons that we love it!

6. Restrict home/work multi-tasking

Multi-tasking has been on the receiving end of some bad publicity recently. Many of us work with multiple screens at the same time: emails, social media, and documents we are working on. I am right now. But word on the street is that this way of working is not efficient or effective. There is downtime for your brain as you switch between tasks and a higher possibility of making errors.

For those of us who work from home there are even more temptations to attempt to add to the list of potential multi-tasking activities. Household chores, running errands, and paying bills are just some of the extra tasks we often try to fit into our day. It's one thing to use the flexibility of working from home to get a few things done, but trying to do all the housework and business-work at the same time can impact your productivity.

If you are working and thinking about the fact that you should be cleaning the shower, you won't be concentrating on your work. And if you're cleaning the shower in your allocated work time you certainly won't be getting much done *(other than have a nice clean shower, which is not helpful if you have a report due!)*.

The flexibility of working from home and being able to throw on a load of washing or unstack the dishwasher can be really helpful. Not to mention something useful that you can do in your breaks. The knack of balancing work and home is to use the flexibility without sacrificing your work productivity.

Here are some tips to help you restrict the multi-tasking between work and household chores:

- Set expectations with the people you live about what you can do around the house when you are working.

- Limit yourself to set household activities during the working day. For example, hanging out the washing or doing a bit of a tidy up *(not the whole house though!)*.

- Outsource… can you make more money spending an hour working rather than vacuuming? If you can afford it, pay someone else to do it.

- Stick to your work schedule so that you have the personal time you need to contribute to your household and avoid being torn between the two.

Pick and choose what is going to be easy for you to do, what absolutely has to be done *(lunch doesn't make itself)* and tasks that you enjoy to break up your day. Just manage your expectations about how many personal things you can do when you are meant to be working. Your home is also your work, so make it work for you.

7. Avoid distractions

The phone, whether it rings or not can be a major work distraction. A 2018 Deloitte survey found that Americans check their phone on average 52 times a day[iv], and Ofcom reported that Brits check theirs every 12 minutes, every day[v]. Talk about a distraction and a drain on productivity!

Then there are the email alerts, meetings, social media, and the need for a coffee. All possible distractions that workers of the world, regardless of where they are located, try and overcome for the sake of efficiency.

Add in the other people that may be home while you are working, the temptation of the TV, the allure of the fridge, the household chores calling your name, and deliveries to the front door… the additional distractions of working from home can be plentiful.

Laura McLoughlin works from her home in Belfast, Northern Ireland, 1–2 days a week and deals with the distractions by locking herself away in her office. She says, *"That way, I don't think about the washing in the clothes basket in the bedroom, or the marks on the mirror in the bathroom. It also helps me get in the right mindset for work, as opposed to sitting elsewhere in the house, which I associate more with relaxing or having time off."*

When comparing working from an office or home, Laura says she finds working from home much more distracting: *"In an office, you are accountable to those around you, but at home, you answer to yourself and yourself isn't always the best boss. Plus, you can actually see all the housework you've left undone and it can niggle at you if you don't shut yourself away from it for the day."*

Sarah who works in the recruitment industry in Sydney, Australia, finds that unless she is super busy it can be easy to be distracted. She deals with this by just pushing herself to work through her to-do list. She advocates focus and balance, particularly when it comes to household chores. *"Try to find a balance that works for you,"* she says.

If you aren't getting through the amount of work that you want or need to do, spend some time working out what is distracting you. Is there a pattern? There might be one main culprit or a number of distractions. Once you work out the source, you can deal with it. If the phone rings constantly and interrupts your work, put it on silent. If emails are distracting you, turn off the notification setting. If you are distracted by social media, limit your time to when you are taking your breaks.

Put some strategies in place to avoid pesky distractions, and stay focused.

8. Include something you enjoy in every day

The New York Times' bestselling author of *It's called Work for a Reason!* Larry Winget talks about the fact that he doesn't love every aspect of his work. He says he loves giving speeches, but most of his time his 'work' is the time he spends traveling. The time he loves being on stage to speak is the payoff for what he 'puts up with' when he travels. *(Based on his colorful description of cabs and airports, travel is something he clearly does not like.)*

Hopefully, you like most of the work you do. But there are likely to be tasks that do not fill your heart with joy. The reality is that some parts of work are hard. Or boring. Or frustrating. Or, worst of all, all three. But they have to be done. They are necessary to enable you to do the part of your job that you do like. The key to getting through or putting up with these unloved aspects of your job is to really enjoy the other parts of your work. The trade-off needs to be worth it.

A lot of people recommend doing something you enjoy every day. For instance, exercise, music or catch-ups with friends. Why not extend this to the working day? And not just something you enjoy, but some part of your work that you *really* enjoy.

What do you enjoy? It could be:

- A type of work you find very satisfying – writing a report or a presentation, or crunching some data to see what it tells you

- A call with someone you genuinely like. They might be funny or inspiring, or you might learn something from them every time you connect

- Completing something that you have worked on for a long time and enjoying an immense feeling of satisfaction when you do

- Making a presentation

- Doing something that is going to make a difference to a customer or colleague.

It's different for everybody. You might be amazed at the suggestion that number crunching can be enjoyable… for some people it is! The crucial thing is for you to understand your most enjoyable activities. And then schedule one of them into your day. Every day.

When you have something to look forward to every day, you may not bounce out of bed in the morning, but it will help you feel positive and enjoy your day. *(I admit, there's not much bouncing out of bed in my house until after coffee, but I do make sure I do something every day that I enjoy!)*

9. Manage time with friends

Kandy Shepherd is a former magazine editor in London and Sydney and now a prolific and award-winning Harlequin Mills & Boon romance author. She has a multitude of friends that she loves to talk to but finds this can be a dilemma when working to a deadline. When she's writing, she needs to limit the amount of time she spends on the phone with her friends.

Family and friends have absolutely no idea if you are under the pump, or whether a call from them would be a welcome distraction. And people who have never worked from home probably don't realize that you have to be disciplined with your time.

Losing valuable time in your day can have a really negative impact, causing missed deadlines, feeling anxious about what you need to do, or like you need to work long into the night.

If you do answer your phone *(and that is discretionary, people!),* politely letting the caller know that you have to get something finished or simply that you are busy and arrange another time to call them back will send the appropriate message and get you back to your work.

It's not just calls either. Texts and social-media messages are often expected to have a fast turnaround for a response. Unless it's urgent, responses can wait. Use one of your breaks, or the end of the day, to respond or let your friends know when you will be able to get back to them.

There can also be the temptation to meet for a coffee or grab some lunch with a friend. This is one of the loveliest perks of working from home and being able to set your own schedule. Just don't do it simply because you've been asked and your friend has time. If you have work you need to do, politely decline or suggest another day. If you can fit it into your schedule, know how long you have allocated and be disciplined about sticking to your time limit.

Managing your time with friends and family doesn't mean placing yourself in seclusion. Just be proactive in managing your time so that it works for you and you can still be productive.

10. Put your phone on silent

Anyone misplaced their phone only to realise that it's on silent mode and you can't ring it to help you find it? Or is that just me? Usually it's buried under papers on my desk or in another room. Once it was inside one of my slippers and another time it was in a kitchen drawer! It always turns up *(so far),* but it's inconvenient when I can't find it.

The reason my phone is often on silent is that it rings when I am working. All the time. This disrupts my concentration when I am deep in the middle of a task. So I switch it to silent mode when I know I am going to get stuck into something, so I don't get interrupted.

I still have the phone sitting on my desk in front of me and on vibrate mode. That way, I can monitor my calls and answer anything that is urgent. I have a number of text responses set up that I can quickly send to let people know I will call them back and check that this suits them. But when a call from an unknown number comes through, it's highly likely that I'll leave it to go to voicemail. Many of these are telemarketing calls and not worth interrupting my workflow to answer.

If you're worried that you might miss something important, like a call from your boss or a key client, most smartphones have a Do Not Disturb function that allows you to assign a ringtone for certain contacts.

Another little-used function on a phone is the conveniently placed 'Off' button. This will actually stop all calls and messages from disturbing you! It might not be an option if you need to always be contactable. But if you can go off the grid for some time while you are working on something super important or complex, this feature will give you some real peace and quiet to concentrate.

To reconnect with the world, all you have to do is turn your phone back on or take it off silent or do not disturb. When you do return your calls or respond to texts or messages, you will be able to focus on them much better. This ultimately is more respectful to your caller as it enables you to give them your full attention.

These are great tools to help you prioritize your time, focus on what is important, and be productive.

11. Turn off email notifications

A ping. A little envelope in the corner of your screen. A big fat pop-up taking over the screen. These are just some of the ways your inbox demands your attention. These enticements to respond instantly to email are distracting, not to mention unnecessary.

You're working on something and you see that an email has come in. You're torn. Do you keep going with what you're working on or just have a quick look at your inbox and see if it's urgent? The time you spend on that split-second decision alone is interrupting your concentration – even if you decide to keep going on the task at hand.

It's estimated that an office worker receives on average 121 emails each day[vi]. That's a lot of potential interruptions in a day.

Learning to turn off these notifications has been revolutionary for me. I got to see *Smart Work* author Dermot Crowley present a whole range of ways to use digital tools to help get focused and prioritize. The one that really stuck with me and has truly made a difference to how I work is turning off these notifications.

Sometimes when I am working, I forget that my email is on and get a surprise when I pop back to find there are a dozen or more new messages. That's 12 times I wasn't interrupted and was able to concentrate on my work.

Of course I am often tempted to check my email *(probably more often than I should)*. I have allocated work time in my diary for email but, I admit, I do check it more often than that. Still, by turning the notifications off, it's just one less *(or maybe 121!)* distraction in my day. And if something is super urgent and you don't respond in six seconds? They'll call. Believe me!

So how do you do turn off those email notifications? It's remarkably easy.

If you are an Outlook user go to File > Options > Mail. Under Message Arrival select or clear the Display a Desktop Alert check box and then select OK. There are also check boxes for playing sounds, mouse pointer changes and displaying an envelope in the task bar. Untick them all!

In Gmail, go to Settings > scroll down to Desktop Notifications > Mail Notifications Off, scroll down to bottom of the page Save Changes. And you're done.

There are different variations for different programs and different devices and they do change with version updates… but you get the idea.

Give it a go. Turn the notifications off and allow yourself to be engrossed in something else. Your email will still be there and waiting for you when you're ready!

12. Limit social media

Yes, that old chestnut. Wherever you turn there is someone telling you to reduce your screen time or stop wasting time on social media. Facebook posts, Twitter feeds and checking the number of likes on your most recent Insta pic are just some of the social-media platforms that could distract you during the day.

Before you reject this tip out of hand, I know there may be a good reason for you to be on your socials. You may actually need to use some of these tools as part of your work for research or to engage with clients. Or you may just be having some time out when you are between tasks. Why not? Your office-bound colleagues are probably chatting with each other in the kitchen or have been hauled into meetings while you have been working efficiently.

And there is some research[vii] that backs up that some personal time online might be good for you with the dopamine system *(the stuff that makes you feel good)* activated by social media 'likes' and online interactions with family and friends. Further evidence of this *(just in case you ever need to argue your case for checking your feeds)* has been provided by University of Melbourne Marketing Lecturer Brent Coker. He released a study in 2009[viii] that found that workplace internet leisure browsing has positive effects on employee productivity, and that the more enjoyable the break, the greater the improvement in productivity.

I would be the last person to say don't use social media during the working day – because I certainly do. The risk is, however, that you'll get sucked in for much longer than you planned, then it's a real time-waster. A quick check of your feed can lead you down the path of cat videos and hilarious quotes. It can be a vortex that sucks you in and leads to panicking about how much time you've lost.

Limiting social media can be the solution. Of course, there's an app for that *(many actually)* if you need some help staying on the straight and narrow. Or monitor the time that you spend and be conscious of not wasting your most precious resource – your time. You've got to like that.

13. Use an out-of-office email response

This took me a little while to figure out, but I just never thought of using an automated out-of-office response on my emails when I was traveling as a work-from-homer. I figured, I'm not usually in the office with other people, so what difference does it make when people don't see me every day anyway?

Turns out it makes a big difference. I travel reasonably often for work, which brings with it the challenges of being offline thanks to being on planes, lots of background noise and, quite simply, being in transit and not able to have confidential conversations. These things all make it difficult to be available to colleagues and customers when you are on the move. Also, I'm not that good at juggling the phone and getting out of a taxi at the same time.

Using an out-of-office response when traveling can take away a big source of stress. As a work-from-homer, people get used to not being able to see you across the office, but they still assume that you will respond in a reasonable time frame. When you travel, you just don't have the same availability. Using an out-of-office reply when traveling, helps set expectations about when you'll be able to get back to the people who are trying to contact you.

It doesn't make the work go away or the emails slow down, but it does help with the pressure of how quickly you feel you need to respond. The same goes for sick days. If you take a day off work because you are not well, don't feel that you should be lying on the couch or in bed responding to emails. Don't be sucked into thinking that just because you are in the same work environment you might just as well do a few emails.

If you are not well, any response you give is unlikely to be your best work. Be fair to yourself, and give yourself time to get better. And be fair to the people who are contacting you and respond when you are able to be clear headed and focused. Put an out-of-office response on your email and look after yourself *(or even better see if you have someone who will look after you – if you do... let them!)*.

And, of course, when you are on vacation it is an absolutely must to have an out-of-office message. It's important so that you get a proper break from work and people contacting you know who to contact or when you will be available – all of which you can include in your automated response. Even if you are having a staycation at home it will be much more of a break if you use an out-of-office response.

What to include

There are a couple of should-haves for your out-of-office reply: an anticipated return date and the contact details for someone else who can help them are minimum requirements. Ideally this should include both an email address and a phone number.

It can be good to include that your access will be infrequent or intermittent *(if you want people to know that you will see their message at some point before you return)*, or that you won't have access until you are back at work. The internet is awash with examples of professional, funny and 'best-of' examples of messages for inspiration.

The most important point is that if your availability is different from normal – due to travel, illness, taking your well-earned vacation or myriad other reasons – don't think that you have to keep up with your regular workload just because your workplace is at your home.

When you are out, be out, and use your out-of-office.

14. Pick up the phone

I know, it sounds shocking but there is nothing quite like the old-fashioned approach of actually talking to someone. What I am suggesting is sending fewer texts and emails and improving your productivity by calling people.

For the texting/instant messaging times we live in, this seems counterintuitive. There's no need for small talk when you fire off a text with a quick question. No need to listen to a long and rambling voice mail message when your contact doesn't answer. But the bottom line is it can be faster, less prone to ambiguity or misinterpretation, and actually talking to your colleagues and clients will help you build relationships with them.

Let's dig into these three benefits a little deeper to see if I can convince you.

Calling can be faster

Okay I'll admit that if you spend 20 minutes chatting about the weather or last night's reality TV show this might not be the case. But even with some light rapport building at the beginning of a call, it can be much faster to sort out an issue with a quick phone call.

It is often easier to provide context to a topic and have a more interactive and valuable two-way communication when you can hear the tone of each other's voices and have the ability to ask questions.

Add to this the fact that we talk at about 110–160 words and type at about 40 words per minute; you can cover a lot more ground in that minute on the phone. It can be much more efficient to make a fast and succinct call. One way to make it clear that you haven't rung for a long chat is to say, *"Hi, I just wanted to give you a quick call to ask about…"* They won't feel like you are going to be a big interruption to their day and it helps you quickly get to the point.

And as an added bonus, if you call instead of email you won't have to respond to the reply! One less email can't be bad, can it?

Less prone to ambiguity

The temptation, particularly if you feel more articulate in writing, is to rely on written communication. However, for anyone who uses the written word there are some hidden dangers. When you write, there is no opportunity to add detail if something isn't clear to the reader. You also don't get to judge the comprehension of your how well your audience has understood your message. And there is always the danger that you'll come across differently to how you intended. A jokey retort in an email may come across as inappropriate or sarcastic to a reader.

With most people receiving many emails a day at work – it's easy to understand how quick messages, sent when you're in a hurry, stressed or thinking about something else, may not be your *(or someone else's)* best literary effort. They can lead to ambiguity or misunderstandings. Even worse is relying on email if you are trying to resolve an issue or discuss a difficult situation. It can be tough but taking a deep breath and making a call can be much more effective and will often be appreciated, or at least respected, by the other person.

Helps build relationships

That appreciation combined with the ability to have a two-way communication will go a long way towards building relationships. People who respect you, will speak well of you and help you out when you're in a pickle. They are absolute assets to your business or career. These relationships can make all the difference to how successful you can be and even whether you get the next job or client you're after.

These kinds of relationships are rarely built through email exchanges. You need to talk to people. This applies to everyone, but for those of us who work from home it's even more important. With no elevator pitches or chitchat in the office kitchen to help build rapport with others, you need to create the opportunities.

Pick up the phone and make some calls.

You might even like it!

15. Find a routine

Scheduling your time, starting the day with a shower, and working in the most productive part of your day – all help form a routine. Walk the dog, take the kids to school, go for a run, take a coffee break… these are just a small sample of the activities that form a routine. This can be helpful to keep you on track with your work.

How? None of these activities involve actually doing work, it's true, but they can help you form routines that will get you focused and working when you need to be.

And that varies for different people. If you have particular hours that you need to be available to work, then your routine will be pretty locked in. If you have flexibility with your working hours, then establishing some habits to help you start and stop work can be important.

James Carpenter has worked for himself as a recruitment consultant for over 20 years. He says working regular office hours is a routine that works for him. Whereas a number of other people I spoke to said they use the flexibility of working from home to work in with their family. They might start work after they take the children to school, take an afternoon break to supervise snack and homework time, then do some extra hours in the evening. They are able to work to a routine that works for them and their family.

Setting an alarm in the morning, scheduling your time and a basic plan for the day can all help keep you on track. Knowing what you need to do and when you are going to do it for both your work and personal life are important. Having a routine can help you stay on track and avoid having to work late into the night or finding that there is no food in the house because you didn't take a break to go to the store.

Of course, a routine can be changed for unexpected opportunities or personal priorities. I've only had one of my besties turn up with a bottle of Champagne in the middle of the afternoon once… but it was a very good afternoon, and I will admit that all work was abandoned for the day. Working from home meant that with a bit of quick rescheduling

I could enjoy the opportunity when it arose. The next day my routine was back to normal, I squeezed in a few extra hours, and I was back on track.

Find a routine that works for you and makes the most of the flexibility of working from home. It helps your productivity and makes your workday more enjoyable.

16. Take breaks

Research supports that taking a break is not only good for you, but also aids your productivity. *Psychology Today* reported that work breaks help your brain by:

- improving health and well-being
- preventing decision fatigue
- restoring motivation
- increasing productivity and creativity, and
- helping consolidate memories and improve learning[ix].

These are potentially significant benefits – even just from activities as simple as getting up from your desk, grabbing a glass of water, and taking a walk outside the house.

But that's not all. In a *New York Times*' article, Associate Professor John P. Trougakos from the University of Toronto Scarborough explained that mental concentration is like a muscle and needs a rest period after sustained use[x].

The question is how often should you take a break? Trougakos said that if you are on a roll you don't have to take a break. But there are others who advocate a stricter schedule.

Francesco Cirillo developed the Pomodoro Technique in the late 1980s, which is based on 25 minutes of work followed by a five-minute break, with a longer break after four of these sessions[xi]. *(Fun fact: the technique was named after a tomato-shaped kitchen timer that Cirillo used when he was developing this methodology.)*

Copywriter, Leanne Shelton finds committing to 20 minute sprints when she's feeling stuck helps her get into the swing of things. Often, time flies by and she's happy to continue working and, before she knows it, she's smashed out a couple of hours of work! Other times, Leanne gives herself a little break when the alarm goes off. She then treats herself to a few minutes of social media scrolling, makes herself a tea, or heads outside for a breath of fresh air.

When she's not out and about in her CBD office, or with clients developing strategy or facilitating workshops, Lyndal Hughes works from her home in Sydney, Australia. Lyndal takes a break for a cup of tea or a glass of water for five minutes every hour. She says she likes to stand in the sun to freshen up, then get back to her desk. *(I can almost hear her take a deep breath as she soaks in the Sydney sunshine!)*

A study by DeskTime observed that the 10% of their users who considered themselves most productive have an average pattern of 52 minutes working and a 17-minute break. The research suggests that the longer break allows you to properly rest and then be fresh for the next work stint, which is then more productive[xii].

And then there's the health and well-being benefits – for which the research is extensive. The Centers for Disease Control and Prevention *(part of the US Department of Health & Human Services)* recommends that regardless of the type of work you do, take five-minute breaks about every hour that include some movement[xiii].

Looking after your eye health as well as weight and stress management and a bunch of other health benefits all seem like pretty good reasons to take a break.

I can't possibly go through all the research here *(I'm due for a break!)*, but the evidence seems pretty overwhelming that both you and your work will benefit if you take a break.

17. Build a virtual team

There is a possibility, however remote it may be, that you are not brilliant at everything. Even if you have not previously considered this before, I'd like you to entertain the possibility that there are things that you do when you work from home that you shouldn't. Not because you can't do them, but because they may not be the best use of your time.

Tasks that your organization has support people to help you with, for example. People who specialize in specific functions because they might be slightly more competent or faster at doing them or just have the luxury of time because this is their job and what they are meant to be working on. If you are running your own business, there are tasks that other people have set-up businesses to do – for people just like you. Even if you have the capability to do a task, do you have the capacity? Is it the best use of your time?

When you work from home it's easy to fall into the trap of being a little too self-sufficient. This can result in spending way too long on stuff you shouldn't, like trying to get the new printer connected or on admin tasks. You may be working from home alone, but you can build yourself a virtual team to help you out with these peripheral activities.

Apart from helping you get stuff done there is the added benefit of having regular contacts that are part of your working life. When you have reliable, helpful virtual-team buddies it can reduce the stress of how much you have to do and provide a regular source of interaction.

The theory behind building a virtual team is the same whether you are an employee of an organization or working in your own business… but the execution will be slightly different.

When you are an employee

Depending on the size of the organization you work for, they may have people who are dedicated to functions that will support you. For instance, IT Help-desks, Human Resources, and Admin people may be at your disposal. They are just not as easy to find when you are not in the office. If you don't know if you can utilize these services, ask your manager. If you come across good, helpful people, make sure you get their name, email and phone number – these people are an invaluable asset to your virtual team.

When you are 'it'

When you have your own business, are a contractor, or part of the gig economy, there is no organization of specialist functions you can access, but there is no reason why you can't build your own virtual team.

Unless you are a computer geek, use a local expert. If bookkeeping and accounts aren't your thing, find other people who love crunching numbers. Spending way too long organizing your diary and booking your travel? Think about a virtual assistant, who would be a wiz at that stuff.

Yes it will cost you money but when you work for yourself outsourcing the time-consuming or frustrating tasks, it frees you up to focus on delivering whatever it is you do. What you get paid to do.

Regardless of your employment arrangements – employee or self-employed – don't do stuff just because you can. Or think you'll eventually figure it out. Don't waste your time on low-value activities.

Build yourself a virtual team and focus on what you *are* brilliant at doing.

18. Focus on success

What does success at work look like for you? It could be writing a comprehensive report, preparing a killer presentation, or signing up a new client. Be clear about what success is for you. To use your work time well *(and not let work sneak into your own time)* it's vital to know what high-value activities will contribute to the outcomes you want to achieve.

You need to know not only what success looks like, but also how you are going to measure that you have had a successful day, week or month.

One of my go-to management books is Stephen Covey's *7 Habits of Highly Effective People*, and my favorite tip in that book is 'Begin with the end in mind'. When you know what you are working towards, it helps you stay focused on what you need to do and set measures to help you get there.

For instance, as I am writing this book I am pretty clear that I need to write up 101 tips for working from home – that's the commitment I made with the book title. *(If you are reading this, then I have been successful.)* I have also set myself some interim targets to help me achieve this goal and some rewards when I get to key milestones. *(I'm looking forward to Tip 40 because my reward is a new pair of shoes!)* All of which are aimed at keeping me on track and focusing on what I want to accomplish.

Customer and employer satisfaction will be higher when you deliver their requirements, which is best achieved by focusing on outcomes. Apart from feeling good about what you achieve, staying focused protects your personal time so you are not wasting work time on low-value activities.

Goal setting

It's highly likely that you have heard of the SMART goal-setting framework: Specific, Measurable, Achievable, Realistic, and Timely. There are a few variations on the words that make up that acronym, but they all add up to the same thing. Be clear about what you want to achieve, make sure it is realistic to measure, and that it can be achieved in a defined timeframe.

The website for Monash University has upped the ante and added two more steps; Evaluate and Record[xiv] *(write them down)*. Which makes the technique SMARTER. Cute. As the Monash site says it's something of a cliché. But I think that's why it works as a simple tool to help you make sure you are clear on your goals.

Real-world examples

A number of work-from-homers recommend using sticky notes as a mechanism to stay focused on what needs to be achieved in a day. Pilot and flight-test examiner Gary Clarke puts up a sticky note for each activity that he needs to complete and then takes them down as he finishes each task. He says, *"It's a great visual tool."*

Working in an entirely different field as the Managing Director of a leadership and strategic-change consultancy service, Lyndal Hughes also uses sticky notes. Lyndal writes down her must-dos for the day and comes back to them regularly to make sure she is staying on track. She also recommends shutting the home-office door even if no one else is home to psychologically block out the rest of your life.

Prioritization is also important. A former colleague and Facebook friend of mine shared that what she doesn't get done in a day gets added to her list for the next day. *"What gets carried over may not have been important today,"* she says, *"but tomorrow it may jump to the top of the list."* Reviewing your priorities is another relatively easy way to stay focused on your success.

Time is precious and finite. Use yours to achieve what will be successful and rewarding for you.

19. Make time to work

It may seem completely obvious and self-explanatory to say you should make time to work. But it is so easy for the day to be consumed by meetings, emails and phone calls. An entire day or week can disappear in responding to the needs and requests of others. The thing that often falls by the wayside is what you need to do: the project deliverable you are on the hook for, the proposal you need to send to a customer, or the calls you want to make.

Senior executive and non-executive board member Justine Cain has incorporated 'Meeting-free Friday' as a regular part of her weekly routine, over the past eleven years, to make sure she gets time to focus on strategic planning, analysis of short, medium and long term data trends and to plan effectively for the following week. Although she primarily works from the office, Fridays are set aside for working from home with no set meetings. Justine's Friday starts very early so she can get at least three hours of work in before having breakfast with her daughter and walking her to school. A ritual that is important to them both. *(Justine is a very early bird and even then does not work in her pajamas!)* Once drop off is done it is "back into it." Friday's are highly productive and are a great opportunity to catch-up with her team and colleagues, without having to cut off important discussions because she has to rush to the next meeting.

Over the years meeting-free Friday has been adopted by many of her teams because they can see how well it works. I have adopted the practice and found that it makes a huge difference to my ability to deliver when I have a whole uninterrupted day to work. There is something liberating about starting on something and knowing that you can keep going and not have to stop at a certain time for a meeting. It also has a benefit during the week because every time you say, *"I'll do that..."* you know that you have some time to actually do it.

Fridays may not work for you. A whole day may not be realistic based on your work. And there are always exceptions to the rule: urgent meetings you have to attend, customers you have to see, people who won't be persuaded to meet you on another day.

However, it is the principle of making time to work and getting through what you need to do that can significantly impact your productivity. Make time for your priorities by making time for your work.

II. WORK VERSUS HOME *(how to keep the balance)*

Combining different elements can have a marvellous outcome. Imagine you are baking a cake. *(I'm thinking of a soft vanilla sponge with whipped cream topped with fresh ripe strawberries, but I digress…)* All the right ingredients, put together the correct way, baked at the perfect temperature and the result is magnificent. Get quantities or timings wrong and you can have a flop on your hands.

When you combine your personal and your professional life under the same roof the outcome can be brilliant. But it can go wrong. Your working day can be interrupted by the demands of your personal life, work can intrude on your time with family and friends, and there is the potential for work to negatively impact the people in your household who are living in your workspace *(and want access to you)*.

A 2017 study by Eurofound and the International Labour Office *Working anytime, anywhere: The effects on the world of work* – looked at research from 15 countries and found that two of the downsides of working from home are the tendency to work longer hours and an overlap between paid work and personal life[i]. The good news is that, overall, the study found that better work–life balance is one of the positive effects!

Like following a recipe carefully, there are some simple strategies to manage the potential downside of having work and home under one roof.

Are there people coming and going from your house at certain times of the day? Don't schedule teleconferences or calls for times you know the children will be stomping through the house. Get distracted by the chores you can see piling up? Outsource. Have trouble separating from work at the end of the day? Leave your laptop in your office.

There is no single magic answer to maintaining the balance between work and home… and their often-competing demands. You need to work out the formula that will work for you.

20. Dedicated office space

A dedicated office space is a very good idea from both a productivity and work/home balance perspective. Everything is set up and ready to go when you start in the morning, so you don't waste valuable time getting organized every day, nor do you encroach on your household by taking over the dining-room table. It's also a cue that when you are in your office you are there to work, which can help minimize the distractions of being at home *(at least you have to get up to go the laundry, coffee machine or fridge)*. And it provides you a quiet area to focus on your work.

All of which are important considerations when you work at home. In addition to this it can be an easy way to separate your work and your personal life.

A dedicated office space can assist you in distinguishing between work and home. Some of the advantages include:

- Sending a signal to other people in the house that you are working.

- Safeguarding the rest of the house for personal use and relaxation – so you don't feel that you are at work all the time.

- Further separating you from your living areas (if there's a door) and providing privacy, and peace and quiet.

- Helping you 'switch off' faster when you are done for the day and close the door behind you.

If you don't have a separate room to work in, create a space and try to replicate the benefits as much as you can. A desk that is in a quiet area and set up with the tools you need *(monitor, stationery, cookie jar... I mean fruit bowl!)*, while not having that all-important door, can still provide a dedicated work area.

If you have to pack up the area – make it as easy as possible to set up and get back into it the next time you start work. A basket of stationery and all your cords can make the pack and set up just a little bit easier.

However, if you work at home and have the luxury of a room with a door, which you can dedicate to work… do it!

And an added bonus is that you can decorate your office the way you want. Your colleagues can't move any of your stuff or object to your choice of interior design (*although think about what's in the frame when you do video calls!*). You get to sit in the same place every day and not have to pack up like the office-bound, hot-desking folk. Just another little bonus of working from home!

The benefits for you and the people you live with will justify the use of the room that you set aside for this purpose. A physical boundary between work and home will help you maintain the balance between work and home.

21. Agree boundaries with your household

Unless you live alone, your home is not just *your* home. You might share it with family, friends or housemates. They might not be there all the time while you are working but chances are they'll be in the house at some stage when you are trying to work.

As the person who is there most of the time and trying to earn a living we know what we need from them. They need to be quiet, not interrupt you *(particularly while you are on the phone)*, not play the TV too loud, and if they bring you the occasional cup of coffee, tea or a snack – that would be an added bonus.

The complication is that it's their home, too, and it has to work for everyone. When someone works from home there needs to be a clear understanding of how the two worlds can work together.

It's imperative to have a discussion and agree how it will work. Your children may not understand why they can't burst in and tell you what just happened to Baby Shark, or ask for help with their homework when you're paying a perfectly good babysitter to look after them… but they will *(mostly)* understand that a shut door means that you are working and shouldn't be disturbed. It's not foolproof but it can help.

A shut door didn't help Professor Robert E. Kelly when his children burst into his office while he was being interviewed live on the BBC about South Korean politics in 2017. Simply not locking his door before going on-air led to the family becoming an internet sensation – and much debate about the challenges of working from home. Things will go wrong from time to time, and that's when you really need to go with the flow of being at home. You might not end up with your call being dissected frame by frame on *The Ellen Show* like the Professor, but handling these kinds of tricky situations efficiently and with a sense of humour is respectful to your family and will, usually, be understood by your business associates.

What to agree on

Setting expectations about the hours that you are going to work can also be helpful. If the people you live with know when you are going to be available it will help them work around your requirements.

Another issue to be clear about is how much household work you will be able to get done in a day. An occasional load of washing or unstacking the dishwasher is one thing. Painting a room or a spring clean is another. An authentic conversation with people who go out to work about what you need to do in your work day will help manage the potentially unrealistic assumption that when they get home from work you will have a three-course dinner on the table *(with no involvement from a meal delivery service!)*.

On the other hand there are some things you can do that will help out your family or housemates and respect their needs. Staying in your dedicated office space when other people are home allows them be free to live in the rest of the house or apartment and not need to work around you. Save the walking while you are talking on the phone or working in the living room for a change of scene to the times when you are home alone.

IT Sales Director Richard Webbe, who mainly works from home, has some tips that work for him. Richard and his wife, who does not work from home, have two small children and family life can be hectic. Richard works around this by not scheduling conference calls or work-focused activities during 'high traffic' times at home. Richard said to me, *"Do not try to do both – work and home work – at the same time. Disaster"*

It just makes sense that when children are going to or coming from school there is going to be more noise than when they are settled doing an activity. Telling them to 'shush' while you are talking to a client is unlikely to be successful. It can remove a lot of stress for everyone if you can schedule your work time or breaks around these peak events.

An adult is unlikely to react any better to children if they are 'shushed' and waved away because you are busy. Even if you only have other adults in the house being present with them to send them off in the morning, say hello when they return, or stop for a coffee with them is a nice way to keep the balance.

Agreeing the boundaries with the people in your house about how you will mix your work with their *(and your)* home life is important for everyone.

22. Create your own commute

The daily commute, which can be time-consuming, stressful, frustrating, and expensive *(or all of these and more)* does have one advantage. It places a space, a segment of time, between work and home.

It's a time to gear up for the day ahead in the morning, and in the afternoon it's a chance to process what has happened in the day and unwind on the way home. A 20-second walk into your home office saves a whole lot of time and stress, but it does not provide a separation between work and home or the chance to think through the day ahead or behind you. Even the Seven Dwarfs had a commute as they set off for work singing, *"Heigh-ho, Heigh-ho, it's off to work we go!" (You've got that stuck in your head now, I bet – sorry!)*

Off to work we go

One of the truly excellent things about working from home is that you don't have to commute and deal with the smelly armpits of fellow travelers or the slow crawl of traffic. You can replicate the advantages of a commute by building a space into your day to help change gears from home to work.

To create your own 'commute' to work and gently enter into your workday, consider:

- Exercise
- Meditation
- Yoga
- Leaving the house to buy a coffee
- Walking out the front door and back in again
- Saying goodbye to the people you live with and letting them know when they can expect to see you again
- Taking the long way home after dropping the kids at school, and

- Establishing a ritual – light some candles, play music, open your windows – whatever you need to set up and get going for the day.

Marketing Manager Serena Varendorff has a well-established process in the mornings to start her day and get productive on the days when she works from home. Once the children have been dispatched to school, Serena says she sets up oils in her diffuser, a large covered water jug, a massive cup of tea and has the air-conditioning pumping. Being based in Brisbane, on the east coast of Australia where it's hot *(and sticky)*, the air-conditioning is a definite requirement!

Honey, I'm home!

At the end of the day I often burst through the door to the TV room with the announcement *"Honey, I'm home!"* This is a signal to my husband *(and I)* that work is over for the day. I attempt a Kramer-like entrance, but never seem to pull it off with the same panache as his entry into Seinfeld's apartment. Still a bit of silliness is a good end to the workday!

Everything on your list to create a commute-like experience in the morning could be used in reverse to signal the end of the day. If you've taken the kids to school in the morning you probably need to pick them up again. *(Schools tend to take a dim view of overnight stays.)* If you exercised in the morning, a nice walk in the evening can be a lovely transition from work to home. Here are some other ideas to signal the end of the workday:

- Turn your laptop off *(do not be tempted to keep having a sneaky peek)*

- Clear your desk – empty coffee cups, water glasses, and abandoned yogurt containers. These will not put you in a productive frame of mind if they are still there the next day

- Shut the door to your office

- Read a book

- Have a bath

- Ring a friend

- Prepare dinner

- Get changed *(there's nothing like some comfy slippers at the end of the day)*.

Do something you enjoy as a reward for the productive or frustrating (or whatever kind of) day you have had.

Creating your own commute through habits and rituals is a good approach to keeping the, sometimes competing, forces of home and work in the same environment in equilibrium.

23. Outsource

Work is getting more and more specialized, expectations are high, and life is short – three very good reasons to outsource what you are not great at, what you don't have time to do, or what you choose not to do. This applies equally to whether you work for yourself or someone else.

Outsourcing work tasks

When you work for yourself, you are everybody. You are the bookkeeper, the appointment maker, the IT department and the cleaner – not to mention whatever it is you actually do to earn money. Chances are you are not an expert in each of these disciplines. And even if you are pretty good at them there is always the question of whether doing non-income earning tasks is a good use of your time.

Would you be better off spending time sourcing a new client or writing up receipts for your accountant? Spending hours trying to make a presentation look snazzy? Or sending it off to a design specialist and moving on to your next piece of strategic work?

Not convinced? Calculate out how much you would earn in the same amount of time you could be paying someone else to do your non-core tasks for you. Estimate how much a new client could be worth to you over time, versus the amount you would save by doing a time-consuming task yourself.

As well as the return on investment equation, you should also consider the quality of the outcome. When you supplement your skill sets with those of others, your finished product will be better. This can enhance your client's satisfaction, your reputation, and ultimately lead to more work.

Even if you work for an organization, this tip still applies. You may not be free to ring the local IT people to come and work on your company computer or outsource your email, but there will be people within your organization who have specialized skills that can help you out. Use their expertise for what they are good at, and devote your precious time to your areas of cleverness.

Outsourcing home tasks

And then there is the cleaning, ironing, after-school care, gardening, lawn mowing, dog walking, bookkeeping, home maintenance and a myriad of household chores that lurk in the background. It doesn't matter how well you schedule your time, you are still stuck with the challenge of only having 24 hours in a day to work with. It's up to you what you do with them!

If you need some justification to outsource some of these household tasks there is evidence that it's a good investment. A 2017 Harvard Business School study, *'Buying time promotes happiness'*, concluded that *"individuals who spend money on time-saving services report greater life satisfaction."*[ii]

Another study of one (*me!*) concluded that I am much happier and able to focus on what I need to do if I am not worried about household tasks. So the research is in, people... investing in help can make you happier!

Sure there are some downsides – like having to lock myself in my office so I don't get in the way of the cleaners, and not scheduling calls when the vacuuming is being done in the hall outside my door – but, all in all, the benefits are more than worthwhile. For my productivity, the personal time I get back, and the peace of mind from not worrying about how I am going to fit everything into my day means I can justify the investment.

You can't buy time

In a 2017 interview, business magnate and CEO of Berkshire Hathaway, Warren Buffet said, *"I can't buy time."*[iii] He added, *"It's the only thing you can't buy."* He can pretty much buy anything else he wants as he is a billionaire. I won't even bother typing how many billions because it will no doubt be more by the time you are reading this.

The point is if you outsource tasks that others can do, you get back time for what is important to you.

Focus on what you are good at, what you like to do and what you have to do – and outsource whatever you can!

24. Signal your availability

'Back in 10 minutes' says the sign on the door to a store when the sole person working there dashes out for a quick bathroom break or to buy an emergency cup of coffee. Slightly annoying if you only had 10 minutes to pick up what you were after, but it's respectful to customers to let them know that someone will be coming back and the maximum *(hopefully)* amount of time you will need to wait. A simple sign stuck to the door might be low tech but it does the job of letting people know what's going on.

Same thing on a plane: put your eye mask on and snuggle under a blanket, and it's a pretty good indicator to the flight attendant that you don't want to be disturbed. Even smartphones have Do Not Disturb mode, so that you can be left alone to concentrate.

Likewise when you are working from home and just can't *(or don't want to)* be disturbed you can signal people in the home environment with some subtle and not-so-subtle 'leave me alone' signs.

Working from home can have all sorts of interruptions like a courier bashing loudly on the door to let you know they have a parcel for you. There have been many times when I've almost jumped out of my skin by the surprise of a sudden, enthusiastic knock on the door. Sometimes this is a welcome interruption to drag me away from the desk, but it's not so good if I am hosting a video or a teleconference.

Bec Bell works as a General Manager for a large corporation, is an Adjunct Associate Professor with a university, and most often works from home in rural New South Wales on a blueberry farm. One of Bec's tips to make her environment work for her is to put a sign out to let couriers and other visitors know that she's not available.

A shut or half-shut door can be an indicator to other people who live in your home about your availability. If you don't have the luxury of a dedicated workspace, wearing headphones, can send a similar message. You don't even have to listen to anything. If you're concentrating on something, noise-cancelling mode works a treat. If you are working in a shared area of the house and you really need to be left alone, let people know you have a confidential call or need to focus on a particular task.

Letting people know when you are not available lets you get on with what you need to do and helps the people around you live around you. And it can take a lot of stress out of the situation for everybody!

25. Limit personal intrusions

Rae is a Senior Account Executive for a major telecommunications company and loves the days she works from home. She says, *"I value the ability to exercise, walk my dog, get my coffee and put a load of washing on, and still be at my office at home at 8.30 am. My dog loves it too and sits beside me."*

But she has found that one of the pitfalls of being at home is the expectation that she is more available to family and friends because she is not in the office. Rae got around this challenge by telling her teenagers that it is still a workday and that she is not available for pickups until after 5pm. They have to wait as if she were in the office.

It's not only teenagers, who might think that 'working from home' means you're available for anything from coffee breaks, grocery shopping, banking and whatever else they can think of! This is particularly true of people who don't or have never worked from home. They don't really get that you have lots of stuff to do, and that you don't get paid if you don't do it. Or that if you take time out of the day you might have to work late into the night.

It's up to you to make the choice. What you don't want is to get 'guilted' into doing things just because you are perceived to be available. This needs to be part of the boundaries you agree with your household. And you might have to have a similar conversation with friends who regularly assume you are available.

This might mean saying no, nicely, to requests that will negatively impact your day and ultimately cause stress or eat into your personal time. *"I'm sorry, I have a deadline / meeting scheduled (or whatever you genuinely need to do), what about…"* and offering an alternative suggestion will usually work and not cause any offence or hard feelings.

Don't feel mean or guilty. Curbing your personal availability when you need to be working will free you up for the times when you don't, and help manage that work–home balance.

26. Agree the plan

In the tip about agreeing boundaries with your household, we talked about discussing and agreeing with your household how things will work. This included setting expectations about the hours you are going to work and staying out of your family's way when they are in the house so that you can happily co-exist.

The people you share your life and home with are so important to the juggle of managing both work and home in the same location that I think it is worth expanding on this idea.

Because it's not just about agreeing boundaries but also developing a plan of how it's going to work – and being explicit about who is going to do what and when they are going to do it. These may seem really obvious but some of the home tasks you might want to agree on can include:

- School drop offs and pick ups
- Cleaning
- Grocery shopping
- Meal preparation
- Laundry
- Gardening
- Walking the dog
- Paying the bills
- Being first on-call for the children's school
- Organizing social activities
- And many, many more!

If it's not agreed, it might be assumed *(very differently by the other parties)* who is responsible for certain tasks. It is easy for others to assume that because you are home you will have picked up the dry cleaning, taken out the trash, fed the cat – and when you don't *(because you are working)*, this can lead to a whole lot of trouble.

The simple way to avoid this is be very clear, even on a daily basis, who will be doing what. If you do have a light workday you could offer to do something extra – pick up groceries, make the dinner early, or let your family know you will be finished early if they want to go for a walk or see a movie.

On the other hand if you have a really full day planned and will be unlikely to even manage your usual household contributions, let people know in advance and set expectations for what you might get done that day. Or on days when your best-laid plans have come undone due to unexpected events and you've done nothing but work, send a text, make a quick call, or take one minute out when others get home to explain what has happened and ask for help. Don't add to the stress of a bad workday by letting tension build if you haven't been able to keep your home commitments. You never know – your significant other may have had a bad day, too. Let them know and you can hatch a new plan or order a pizza.

My father always used to quote this line from a famous poem: *'the best laid schemes of mice and men...'* He would trail off to imply the rest of the line, which translates as *'often go awry'*. Plans often do; it's how you handle them that counts. Having a plan, adapting it, trading off chores, or laughing about mice and men will help keep the peace at home.

Agree the plan of how you will work and live: talk about it, review it, adapt it, throw it out and start again if you have to. The important thing is to identify what needs to be done, plan as best you can, and strive to make it work for everyone in your home.

27. Leave your device in your office

The option to work sitting in the garden, at a café or pretty well anywhere we want is one of the tremendous advantages of working from home. We have the freedom to work where and how we want. This provides the opportunity to soak in some sunshine and fresh air, sit over our favorite coffee or just enjoy a change of scenery. It allows us to juggle work and home simultaneously if you need to be on the sideline of a football field and responding to an urgent issue at the same time.

However, the boundaries between work and home can easily become blurred. When your device is nearby it is just so tempting to 'keep an eye' on the new emails dropping into your inbox or do 'one more thing' before you quit for the day. This is something to really be aware of and manage when you are working from home.

The study I mentioned earlier by Eurofound and the International Labour Office[iv] on the impact of the telework and the transformation of technology in the work environment found that there are both positive and negative effects on work–life balance. With the negative impacts including *"an increase in work hours, a blurring of the boundaries between paid work and personal life and more work–life interference,"* resulting in *"increased work-family conflict."*

One of the contributing factors to this is being 'always on', due to the accessibility provided by mobile devices and smartphones. They give you freedom to work where you want but they also keep you tied to work. The downside is that this can extend the length of your working day, creeping into the time that you need for rest and relaxation, or preventing you from being present with people around you. This is something that needs to be proactively managed!

One of the best tips I have found to deal with this is to leave my devices in my office. The laptop is logged off, closed down and left in the office. When you leave an office and go home you can't see what's happening at work. It provides a very real, physical separation between work and home *(even if you are still checking your phone).*

Walking away and leaving your device in your office or dedicated workspace can help provide the same separation when you work from home. Not only is it physically harder to keep working if you have to deliberately go and get your device, it also provides a real cue that you are finished for the day, which can help you switch off and let go of work. *(And it won't be sitting beckoning you to log on before you've had your coffee and dispatched your loved ones to work or school the next morning.)*

To help maintain the boundary between work and home, when you finish work for the day leave your devices in your office. All of them!

28. Pack up for the weekend

Before you flick over this tip, thinking *"That's fine if you don't have to work over the weekend – this tip is not for me,"* stick with me.

Of course there are times when weekend work is required. Sometimes there are massive deadlines or you've used the flexibility of working from home to take some personal time out during the week and plan to catch-up over the weekend. For the entrepreneur or small business person the weekend can be the only time available to 'manage' your business with invoices, customer quotes and marketing just some of the many activities that you might need to do.

The intention of this tip is not to tell you to take weekends off *(although that is not a bad idea),* but whenever you have a break from work – be it the traditional 'Saturday, Sunday' weekend or another variation of days (or hours) – when you work from home it helps to have a few ways to separate from work. This is taking the previous tip to leave your device in your office at the end of the day one step further.

I have found that locking my work laptop in a filing cabinet for the weekend is liberating. It helps me switch off work for the week, and I don't feel that it is calling me to log on every time I walk past.

I also pack up my client files and put them away. When I do this, it is a good chance to quickly review where I am at and write a to-do list *(or a hastily scrawled sticky note with reminders)* to prioritize the most important things I have to do when I'm back at work on Monday morning.

Whenever it is that you get the chance to take a break – pack up and put the reminders of work away. And as we say in Australia: *"Have a good weekend!"*

29. Let people know when you're done for the day

Separating work and home is not just a challenge for those of us who are working from home, it can also be tricky for the people who live with us. *"Are they on the phone? I wonder what time they are finishing today? Is it okay to turn the TV up?"* are just some of the many questions that may be on the minds of the people in our household who are trying to work around us. *(Personally I'm hoping for "Would she prefer red or white?")*

Letting people know when you are finished working for the day not only helps you separate from work for the day, but also reduces the ambiguity for the people you live with about whether they are in your place of work or their home.

For our friends who don't work at home there is often a text or a call to let others know they are on the way home. Or they walk in the door and call out that they are home. We need something similar and an announcement that you are finished work can help with the balance of work and home life.

It's a signal to everyone that it's okay to talk to you about non-work related topics, make some noise or ask for your help with homework/dinner/or whatever else they have been saving up for you to *'get home'*.

Declaring the end of the working day is an acknowledgment to both yourself and others that you are done – and it's now time to focus on home life.

This is one small habit that can assist in putting some boundaries around your work.

30. Train your colleagues

Whether they are colleagues, customers, staff or business associates, your work contacts seem to develop a sixth sense about the best time to get you – actually, it's usually the best time for them! In my case, this is often between 5pm and 7pm; people invariably tend to ring me when they are on their way home.

Chances are they called you once at a time when you were available but trying to get some work done and you picked up, rather than letting the call go to your voicemail. If you said, *"That's fine, I'm still working"* or mentioned that you work from home in conversation one day, it doesn't take long before you start getting regular calls at that time of day.

The problem is that this might be one of the most productive parts of the day when you are creative and focused. If you lose this valuable time, it can have a real impact on how much you get done. Alternatively, if you have decided to clock off for the day it can start to intrude into your personal time. It's hard enough to manage the boundaries between work and home without others deciding that because you work from home you are available 24/7.

The intrusion into home life can be early-morning calls when there are children to be fed and dispatched to school, or during precious time that has been put aside for exercise or meditation. There are always exceptions to every rule. Times when business priorities will outweigh personal plans, and you will want, or need, to take calls at any time of the day or night.

But there are ways to train your colleagues and contacts about your availability, so you can protect your precious personal time. Here are some ideas:

- Don't answer the phone. Text back to see if the matter is urgent: *"Sorry I missed your call. Do you need me to call you back tonight or is first thing in the morning okay?"* This type of response allows for urgent matters, but if it happens a couple of times it will subtly indicate that you are not always available to pick up the phone out of hours.

- If you are going to be unavailable for a good chunk of time, say, a half day or more, use an out-of-office reply on your email and record a voicemail message that says when you will be available.

- Let people you work with frequently know about your routine – such as what time you usually get back from school drop off/ exercise/or other activity. *"9am is a good time for our next call as I am back from the school run by then"* or *"I need to be finished by 5pm on Thursdays"* will give your contacts some guidelines for working with you.

The people you work with *(or most of them anyway)* are not mind readers. They can't know if it's a good or bad time to call unless you give them some indication.

The other thing that is important is to also be respectful of others' time. The flexibility of working from home might mean that you're pounding on the keyboards at 7am. But just because you have a brainwave before everyone else has had their first coffee of the day doesn't mean it's a good time for you to ring them. Our poor office-based compatriots have lives and commutes that they need to deal with as well. It goes both ways.

It comes down to good old communication. Talk to people about what works for you, be flexible when you need to, and you will be helping your colleagues and clients work out how to work with you.

31. Develop strategies to combine work and home

When you work from home, the reality is the dog will bark, the children will be noisy when they get home from school, and there will be distractions. There is always the temptation to do one more thing or think of something else that you could/should do for work. Your devices and work area are there to lure you back to work every hour of the day or night.

People who work from home have various strategies to work around these encroachments. Sales Director Richard Webbe recommends not scheduling conference calls or activities that require a lot of focus during 'high traffic' times. This reduces the stress for everyone in the household.

Nicole McMahon, a senior IT executive, says working from home allows her to focus on the outcomes and gives her the opportunity to be more organized. She has successfully made a birthday cake while on a five-hour conference call – although it did require the use of the mute button to mask the sounds of baking. She says that button is essential when working from home particularly when there is a naughty puppy in the background! Household noises are a reality and you just need some tools to manage them.

Or disclose what is going on. I quite often walk around the neighborhood while I am on calls *(otherwise my daily step count would be about 13)*. In the late afternoon, the Corellas *(a very noisy species of Cockatoo)* squawk particularly loudly, and I often get asked, *"Is that birds in the background?"* "Yes," I say, *"I am out walking while we talk"* and people are fine with that. *(Not quite sure why, but they rarely raise the topic again!)*

During one memorable meeting I was in a boardroom with a group of people and there was just one attendee who had teleconferenced in from their home. We all looked at each other in shock when he was presenting and was interrupted by a sudden cry followed by *"Get out of here!"* I swear it sounded like a baby. Fortunately there was much relief and laughter all around the table when the presenter came back on the line: *"Sorry, that was the cat crawling on my keyboard!"* No mute button was going to help that situation; confession was the only strategy to deal with that particular overlap of work and home.

Blending work life and home life is also helped if you are realistic about how much you can do in a day. You don't have a commute, but there are still multiple interruptions, from phone calls, meetings and emails to the time it takes to get responses from other people. These, along with being a little too ambitious, can all impact how much you get done. It's not just about your capability, but your capacity. Expect too much of yourself and you will find yourself working long into the night or getting up ridiculously early. Be sensible about what you commit to delivering and what you expect of yourself.

Like I said, if you work from home you work from home. Understand the potential areas of conflict or crossover, recognize them as they happen *(take a deep breath),* and develop some strategies to mitigate the areas of stress for you, your work and your home.

III. WHERE YOU WORK *(how to be comfy)*

One of the best things about working from home is that you get to create your own surroundings. There is no hot-desking and no need to wander around the office to find a place to sit every day. No open-plan seating with no privacy and a bonus serve of noisy co-workers. *(Full disclosure: I am a very noisy co-worker.)* Sure the neighbor mowing the lawn during the middle of the day can be annoying, but you can shut the window and take control of your environment when you are in your own home.

On the other hand, there is no health-and-safety approved, ergonomically appropriate, temperature-controlled work area provided for you. It's up to you to set yourself up so that you can be safe, look after yourself and be comfortable. And importantly, be happy with the space where you are going to spend so much time working.

In this section we look at setting up your office, with the correct lighting and temperature, as well as what to look for in a chair and how to set-up your workstation. We consider what your requirements might be for insurance, a shredder and lockable storage.

And then there is the fun stuff. Stocking up the cupboard with stationery and whatever other bits and pieces you may need *(or in my case think you might need),* which is practical *(well, that's what I tell my husband as yet another batch of pens and pretty notebooks arrive at our door).*

You can create your own space to be as functional, fun or creative as you choose.

The reward for having to do all these things for yourself is that you get to make where you work exactly how you want it to be.

32. Lighting

When we talk about setting up an office we usually start with our chair set-up, desk and the position of our computer. Additionally, the right lighting is important as it can make your home office warm and inviting, or dull and depressing. Issues such as glare, insufficient and poorly distributed light can be addressed not only through lighting solutions, but also through the placement of your desk and computer monitor. They are all in the same room and impact the utility and ambience of your office.

Lighting can impact your mood, productivity and health. Both too harsh and too dim lighting can cause eyestrain and headaches. The right light can make a room warm and inviting. *(Given the number of hours we spend working, I vote for the latter!)*

To make a comfortable and productive environment there are a few different kinds of lighting to be considered: natural, general (overhead), task, and accent lighting. Here are a few things to think about...

Natural lighting

There's a reason why the cubicle near the window is always the first to be snaffled in a traditional office. Apart from a view, the natural light of the window seat helps us see what we are doing. And if you are looking for some scientific justification why this is important for your office *(just in case you need to explain to others in your household why you need the room with the best lighting for your office)*, Psychology Today reported on a study that concluded *'There is a strong relationship between workplace daylight exposure and office workers' sleep, activity and quality of life.'* [i] That's good enough for me!

Take advantage of natural light and manage direct sunlight at different times of day or in different seasons with adjustable blinds, or by moving your desk or computer monitor.

General (overhead) lighting

This is often the main source of lighting in a room and may be needed to supplement natural light on a gloomy day.

The Canadian Centre for Occupational Health and Safety advises not to sit with a light fixture directly behind you when you are working.[ii] *(This is exactly how I am working at the moment as I have relocated to the spare room while my office is being repainted, and I just realised that I am squinting. It's not good – so this is going to be a short tip… actually I'll just go get a lamp for some task lighting.)*

Task lighting

Floor and table lamps are a supplementary source of lighting to help with reading, writing, and computer work. Consider where you place them so you don't have to put up with too much glare or too many shadows over your work.

Not only do they do the job of providing the lighting you need, an adjustable lamp can be moved around to cater for different activities or times of day, which may impact how much extra light you need.

One tip for desk lamps (to help with the shadow) is to place them on the opposite side to your dominant hand. So if you are right-handed, the desk lamp goes on the left. Lefties, you've got it – your lamp should be placed to your right.

Lamps are also a fabulous fashion accessory for your office that can contribute to creating a space you'll love.

Accent lighting

You might want to add some decorative lighting, such as a spotlight for a picture or a wall light, to highlight a feature of your room. This can really help make your office an inviting environment that you want to spend time in.

Turn down the glare

Glare can come either directly from a light source or be reflected by other objects in the room. There are a number of ways to control glare, including:

- using adjustable blinds and lamps to change angles

- installing dimmers on light switches to allow you to turn down the light intensity

- painting walls in light, matte colours to reflect indirect lighting *(one of the reasons my office is being repainted)*

- using a glare protector on your screen.

Set your lighting up so that you are able to work at your most productive, without causing any eyestrain.

And if it makes your office more inviting – that's an added bonus.

33. Temperature

One of the best things about being in charge of your own environment is that you don't have to negotiate with any co-workers about the temperature in the office. You also don't have to wait for the building to heat up or cool down on a Monday morning after the air conditioning has been off all weekend. And you don't need to ring the building manager to get adjustments made.

According to the Helsinki University of Technology, Laboratory for Heating, Ventilating and Air-conditioning, 71.6°F (22°C) is the perfect temperature for the typical office[iii]. In the United States, the US Occupational Safety and Health Administration recommends between 68°F and 76°F[iv] (20°–24°C) which is the same range stated in many building leases in Australia. *(A little fun fact I thought you might be interested in. Or not.)*

Regardless of what the experts say, it seems that half the people in any office are always too hot and the other half are too cold. It doesn't matter when you're at home because you're in charge!

Think about whether you need to invest in some heating or cooling to make yourself comfortable. There are a lot of options, including insulation, air-conditioning, a heating system or even eco-friendly fingerless gloves.

Consider the room you are using and what you need to be comfortable. And remember you get to decide how cool you want to be!

34. Chair

Invest in a good chair. Your butt, back, and neck will thank you. This is really important if you are going to be seated for any length of time.

Even if you have a stand-up desk, there's a strong likelihood that you will be lowering it at some stage and be sitting for long periods of time. Being productive, avoiding injuries and maintaining good posture are all reasons a decent chair is part of being comfy and helping you look after yourself. Grabbing a chair from the dining room is not going to meet any of those requirements.

When I started research for this tip I couldn't believe how much information is available about chairs. Given you have responsibility for Properties and Procurement for your home office, here are some of the most important things to look for:

- support for your lower, middle and upper back
- adjustable height so that you can tailor it to you and your desk
- a tilting mechanism to support you as you recline
- a seat that's about one inch (2.5cm) wider than your hips on both sides so that you don't sit too far forward
- a swivel mechanism for ease of movement within the chair
- arms and headrest (good for when you want to sit back and read), and
- a well-padded back and seat so you can't feel the structure beneath.

And while you're out shopping for a new chair, why not pick up a footrest, too?

If you're a little vertically challenged *(like me)* a footrest provides additional support to keep feet flat and weight distributed. But apparently they're good for everyone to help with circulation and proper posture.

A good chair and a footrest will help make you and your home office comfy.

35. Setting up your workstation

There are quite a few things to think about when you set-up the area where you work. Like having a decent chair, your workstation set-up is all about making sure you don't do yourself an injury, cause your body unnecessary stress, and are able to work as comfortably as you can.

When you work from home, no one from the Health and Safety committee will be there to stop you lying on the couch with your laptop balanced on your knees or sitting on the floor with a million pieces of paper spread around you. But these are not great options for the many hours you are likely to be toiling away at your desk.

Here are a few things to consider for how you set-up and arrange your work area:

Chair

This is where to start to ensure you will be sitting correctly and comfortably. You can adjust everything else in your workstation once you have your chair set-up properly.

Adjust your chair so that you can:

- have the underside of your elbows at desk height (adjust the height)
- sit with your feet flat on the floor (or on a footrest)
- sit up straight (adjust the backrest angle and height), and
- have your arms resting comfortably on the desk (position the armrests).

Your forearms should also be in line with the desk if you are using a stand-up desk.

Desk

Your desk needs to be:

- big enough for all the stuff you need to put on it that's used regularly

- high enough so that your legs fit underneath it and you can position your arms correctly.

It's even better if your desk has:

- convenient storage
- rounded edges, and
- the option to make it a stand-up desk.

Keyboard

The item you are most likely to be using the most on your desk is your keyboard. This should be placed close enough to the front of the desk so that you don't need to stretch and your upper arms stay at your side. Also check that the height of your desk allows your wrists to be straight.

Mouse

Your mouse should be placed as close to your keyboard as possible to avoid stretching, and it should be at the same height as your keyboard.

I personally prefer a wireless mouse, as it is one less thing to get tangled and take up precious desk real estate. And get one you like. I've read quite a few recommendations for vertical shapes because they allow you to support your hand in a relaxed position. *(Based on the number of times I have had to buy a new one at airport tech shops I would also recommend having a spare one for when you travel. And leaving it in your laptop bag! If only I would learn...)*

Monitor

Your monitor should be positioned so that:

- it is directly in front of you
- the top of it is at eye level or just a bit below (you may need to invest in a monitor stand to get it to the right height)

- there is at least a 20" (51cm) gap between your eye and the monitor[v] (*that's about an arm's length*), and

- glare is reduced by having it placed at an angle to windows or by tilting the screen itself. Another option is to have adjustable blinds to deal with the glare.

Look after these basics and you will be set up and ready to work as productively and safely as possible. And you'll be comfy to boot!

36. Stock up on office supplies

I love stocking up the stationery cupboard with supplies. Firstly, because I just love stationery: the perfect pen to hold, an abundant supply of sticky notes, and a rainbow of highlighters. Bliss!

Secondly, there is nothing more annoying *(okay there is, but this is super annoying)* when you don't have the office supplies you need. Need to send something to a client and you've run out of stamps? Annoying. An urgent deadline to print something for a meeting and the printer ink runs out? Potentially disastrous.

Even in this paperless era, you might want at least modest supplies of these items:

- pens
- highlighters
- printer ink cartridges
- printer paper
- sticky notes
- notepads
- folders
- a hole punch
- folder dividers
- scissors
- a label maker
- pencils
- sticky tape

- a pencil sharpener
- stamps
- envelopes
- batteries
- USB sticks
- paper clips
- bulldog clips
- a calculator
- a paper guillotine
- a ruler, and
- a stapler.

Now I am not in any way suggesting that you should limit yourself to this list or that it is any way exhaustive, but this is what a quick stocktake of my stationery cupboard revealed. *(Actually now that I have had a good look I think I might just need a few more Moleskine notebooks – they look very professional for client meetings!)*

37. Shred it!

No, I am not talking about the guys and gals at the gym who are pumping iron and losing body fat. This is about paper. Documents that have commercially confidential or information that is private to your clients, your employer, your business or to you.

When you work in an office, it's usually a short walk to the closest security bin or paper shredder. They are just there. When you work from home you need to think through this trash too.

There are all sorts of paper shredders that have different security levels based on the final particle size. The higher the number; the smaller the particle size; the greater the security. For my purposes I want to minimize the chance of identity theft and protect the privacy of the information that I am working on. I try not to print too much, but when I do, I shred it when I don't need it any more.

There are plenty of different varieties available at office supply stores. One that is often recommended is the cross-cut (also known as confetti-cut) shredder as you end up with many tiny pieces. Another option, if you don't want to go to the expense of buying one for yourself, is that many of these stores offer a high-security document-shredding service, so this might be worth checking out in your local area.

Shredding can be a quite therapeutic activity for a break from work or an excuse to sit in front of the TV while you're protecting your confidential information. Win–win!

38. Lockable storage

Whether it's a filing cabinet, a safe or a drawer in your desk – lockable storage is a great idea for your home office. It gives you an extra layer of security for confidential documents, and when you pack up for the weekend, you know that your laptop is safely tucked away.

Your boss or your client, as the case may be, will also appreciate that their information is safe.

A fireproof lock box will do double duty in protecting your important documents or USB devices in the worst-case scenario of a fire. I work with a client who lost her entire house in a bushfire a few years ago. All she was left with was a suitcase full of winter clothes, as she was away when it happened, and the precious possessions she had tucked away in a storage facility earlier because a bad bushfire season had been forecast. Taking precautions paid off!

My goddaughter and her brother once locked red velvet cupcakes in a hotel safe *(what could be more important?)* and changed the pin code so many times to keep each other away from them that they *(or the safe)* got confused. This resulted in a call to hotel security to have their cakes rescued. The kids thought it was hilarious – not so much laughter from hotel security. Or their parents, given all of their passports were also in the safe. Just goes to show that we all have a different definition of precious! And it is a reminder that you may want to think about an extra set of keys and securely storing your PIN numbers as part of your business-continuity planning!

Lockable, potentially fireproof, storage is a must for security and protection of important information and assets when your office is in your home.

39. Insurance

Now this is one that you are going to need to check out for yourself, depending on your circumstances. I won't give advice on what insurances you might need, I'm just including this tip so that it is on your radar.

If you are running your own business hopefully you are well across what you need as far as liability insurance, public liability, property, business equipment or other forms of insurance that are standard for many businesses. If you're not, speak with an adviser who can point you in the right direction.

Remember to check that any extra equipment you may have bought for your office is covered and that there are no exclusions. If you work for a company, it's well worth checking with your employer to see what their insurances cover you for.

Then there is the matter of whether you need to insure your highly mobile and, therefore, easy to misplace devices, like your phone or laptop. And you might want to consider travel insurance when you are on the road or in the air.

Boring topic? Yes. One that could give you peace of mind? Yep. Something you need to look at? Absolutely!

40. Create your space

At home there is no corporate colour scheme. No bans on personal items on your desk or company-approved only artwork for your walls. You can decorate your space any way you want.

You can create a space to inspire you, make you feel productive, calm or just plain happy. Whatever you need! It's a nice way to start work for the day when you like your work area and can enjoy being in it for the, no doubt, many hours you work.

Marissa, an Account Manager who works from home 1–2 days each week, says she likes to decorate her space with inspiring images. Health and well-being expert Duncan Young advocates bringing nature indoors with either indoors plants or images of nature into your office. This he says not only looks great but also has a biophilic effect. This is essentially about promoting well-being (and feeling good) through connection with the natural environment.

Here are some ideas for what to add to make it your own space:

- Art *(why not a gallery wall?)*
- Cushions – great for comfort, color and something to throw or cuddle *(depending on what kind of day you are having)*
- A rug and/or throw blanket for warmth and colour
- A lamp that you love *(and that does double duty as practical lighting)*
- Pictures of places and people you love
- Baskets for their look and added storage
- A mirror to reflect the outdoors *(or a quick check of how you look before a video call)*
- A clock *(both decorative and practical)*
- A board with images, notes, reminders or mementos.

There are so many 'looks' you can go for: Bohemian, Scandinavian, French Provincial, Industrial, Modern. Or you may just want to add a mat, so that your four-legged friend can hang out with you for some *(or all)* of the day. Whatever you choose!

It is your space, so make it the way you want.

Author's note: For those of you who are playing along at home and reading these tips in order, the shoes (my own personal reward for reaching Tip 40) have been duly ordered!

41. Bits and pieces

There are some other bits and pieces, odds and ends, which you may want to consider for your home office. These additional items could help make your working life a little easier and more comfortable.

Headphones

Whether it's to block out the noise of the neighbours, listen to your music, or avoid straining your neck while you are typing and talking – a quality pair of headphones is worth consideration.

They will need to have a decent microphone so that you can be clearly heard on calls. And they need to be comfortable for those long meetings… If the budget can stretch to it, look at noise-cancelling ones to block out background noise. Mine are an absolute must-have, particularly when I travel.

Whiteboard

A whiteboard is really useful for notes and reminders, a priority to-do list, or working out a problem or designing a process. Standing and writing or drawing with coloured pens *(just make sure they are whiteboard and not permanent ones!)* can give you a break from sitting at the computer for endless hours and stimulate your thinking.

I have mine hanging on the back of my office door so that I can see it when I am working, but I don't have to look at reminders of what I need to do *(or should have done)* when I walk past the room when I am off-duty.

Multi-function printer

Unless you are 100% paperless, there is a strong chance you are going to need a printer. If so, a multi-purpose device will tick lots of boxes. Not only will it print, but also scan and copy documents. There are also versions that include fax capability. It saves a lot of time if you can do these functions from home.

Water glass and coffee cup

A glass that you love the shape of, perhaps a jug for a regular supply of water, and a coffee cup that you adore are lovely additions for your desk and useful, too!

I am sure there is no end to the equipment and miscellaneous paraphernalia that you could buy for your office. The trick is to work out what you need for the type of work that you do, the amount of time that you will be working from home, and how much you want to spend.

Enjoy making your workspace safe, productive and comfy!

IV. TECHNOLOGY *(how to geek)*

Information Technology and Telecommunications make working from home possible. *(They also make watching cat videos, venting on Twitter, and all sorts of other things we would once never have dreamed of possible, too!)*

But back to work. You can see colleagues and clients via video conferencing, work on documents with them through sharing applications, and perform pretty much the same tasks that were once only possible in an office environment.

To enable this capability you do need your office at home to be set up with the technology that will allow you to be as productive as possible, and provide you and the people you work with a good experience.

Some of the things to consider are the speed of your connectivity and what your Plan B is when things don't work as they should. *(Come on, I can't be the only person whose internet drops out in the middle of an urgent customer requirement. And don't get me started on passwords that don't synchronize on all your devices!)*

When you are in charge of your home office, you are responsible for not only your environment as the Fire Warden and Health and Safety Officer, but also business continuity, risk management and disaster recovery.

This needs a plan and some precautions like backing up your work and considering storing documents in the cloud, having security software do its thing automatically, and regularly updating your systems.

You don't need to be a technology guru to work from home – you just need to know what to ask to get one to set it up for you.

42. Fast connectivity

You want to have the fastest internet speed you can afford. Speed is important for video calls, watching video and working with large files, especially if they have lots of graphics. It will allow you to work productively and remove the annoyance of watching the internet wheel of frustration as you wait for pages to upload.

Based on my research, the minimum speed you are looking for is 8 Mbps download and 1.5 Mbps upload[i]. I can't even pretend to be able to explain what this means, but I've provided a link if you want to read more about it. This is what the 'experts' say is required to be able to have good quality video.

Depending on what other applications you use, you may need much more than that – particularly if you are working off an organization's network. Ask the IT folk at your company what speed you need, and they should be able to advise you. For consultants and small-business people, it may take a little research to find out what you need based on which programs and applications you are using.

Apart from the speed of your internet connectivity also consider:

- The reliability of the service – what the guaranteed service levels are in the contract?

- Customer service – how easy is the provider to deal with when things go wrong? And how responsive are they?

- Cost – including monthly charges, contract terms and if there are any cancellation fees.

As a user *(not a tech expert, clearly)* I want a speed that will work reliably and faster than I really need so the technology is waiting for me to keep working, not the other way round.

The need is for speed, reliable speed.

43. Plan B for IT

It doesn't matter how reliable your internet connection or IT equipment is – things go wrong. Having a Plan B or a contingency plan for your connectivity will allow you to keep working when there is an unfortunate event or interruption. This interruption could be internet or power. Or both.

When a massive thunderstorm hit one Friday night, I thought the biggest issue was going to be how wet we would get running back to the car after a bite to eat at a local restaurant. But it turned out that was not the biggest concern for the evening. A house on our street was hit by lightning and we had no internet. For six weeks.

The house and the people in it were fine. Their computer, not so much. Fortunately, our devices were all okay, but the lack of internet was more than a little bit tricky. I will freely admit that my first anxiety was about lack of Netflix *(in my defence, it was a Friday night!)*, but I soon realized that work was going to be an issue.

After a few days our internet provider came to the party with a modem that worked off the mobile network, but until then I was able to get by with a mobile-broadband modem that I had as emergency backup. This meant I was able to work from the Monday morning – without skipping a beat. *(Sadly, due to the cost this was only used for work not movie watching.)*

Some of the things you might want to consider for your backup plan are:

- having a mobile broadband device on hand
- using the Wi-Fi hot spot on your smartphone
- accessing free Wi-Fi networks at a local store or restaurant – although this may not be an option for security reasons if you are connecting into your organization's network (check with the IT Department)
- working from the office or your client's premises

IV. TECHNOLOGY **81**

- charging your phone, laptop and other devices from your car
- borrowing your neighbour's Wi-Fi *(with their permission, of course!)*, and
- breathing deeply and waiting it out *(not really a plan but it may be required!).*

If you work in a remote or regional location, you might also want to think about backup power options.

You might want to consider alternatives for a backup laptop, for example, keeping an old one running and making sure it has updated security software. Equipment repairs take time and your work might not wait while you get someone in to fix it or organize a visit to your local computer-repair place.

There is no IT helpdesk at home to come to the rescue when things go wrong. It's up to you to manage your ability to keep working in case of connection or device failures.

Have a Plan B for your IT.

44. Store documents in the cloud

When you store your documents in the cloud they are not magically transported to one of those fluffy white condensed water vapoury things that float high above us in the sky. *(If they were, wouldn't all your documents get wet when it rained?)* When your stuff is stored on the cloud it's still stored on actual servers, or a number of servers, by your provider. Fortunately, we do not need to be experts in how server farms and such actually work.

What we do need is the ability to access our information from anywhere, anytime; as long as we have internet connectivity. This means that should something disastrous happen to your laptop or other device *(or even your home itself)* you will be able to access your work.

It also reduces the risk of a security, privacy or confidentiality breach as you don't have to carry around information on a memory drive. And it allows you to be flexible as you can work from different devices at different times, and share files with colleagues or customers.

If you work for a company there may be security restrictions that mean you don't have the option to store information out of their network. But usually that means you are storing the information on the company's server – so the information is safe and secure and able to be accessed from different devices and locations.

For the small-business peeps, the freelancers, entrepreneurs, and the rest of us who work from home, the cloud provides storage capacity, reduces business risk, and backs up your data – just one less thing to worry about.

If you currently save information to wish lists or have email on web-based services you are already using the cloud (that is, remote data storage, where someone else is looking after the power, the cooling, the location and the maintenance of where your information is being held).

Thinking about your work bobbing along in a white fluffy cloud in the sky may be a nicer image than it being in a warehouse in the desert with rows of servers, so if you would like to keep thinking of the cloud that way – please continue. However, you choose to imagine it – consider the benefits of farming out the security and backup of your work. *(And don't forget to be super vigilant with your passwords.)*

45. Backup your work

Unless you want to do the same work more than once, or lose valuable information that you would take hours to reconstruct, backing up your files is essential. Power failures, internet outages, device issues, and even the accidental closure of a document without saving it first can all cause hours of work to disappear.

Apart from the loss of your precious time, losing valuable or confidential work can also have a pretty gloomy effect on your credibility. If your boss or client can't trust you to use your time well and protect their information it will not reflect well on you.

When you work on a company network there are often automatic backups built into programs. You just need to check to see how often documents are saved and whether you need to adjust your settings.

For everyone else, putting some measures in place and getting into the habit of saving what is important is worth the investment in time and money.

Some options to consider for backing up your work, include:

- Setting programs to autosave every x minutes *(x being whatever you can bear to lose)*
- Installing a program that automatically backs up your files
- Saving regularly to an external hard drive
- Storing a copy of your external hard drive off site or, if you have it, in fireproof lockable storage
- Emailing files to yourself if your email is on the cloud and your storage is not
- Backing up your documents to the cloud, and
- Backing up your entire PC.

Technology is developing so fast that there are probably even more options available as I am typing this sentence. Whatever you choose to do to help you maintain business continuity and credibility – make sure you do it!

46. Video conferencing

To have a positive video-conferencing experience and make them effective communication forums you may need to get some specialized equipment. Not just rely on whatever is built into your laptop.

A video conference is the next best thing to a face-to-face meeting and allows you to build rapport and grow your reputation. This is going to be undermined if the person or people you are talking with or presenting to can't hear you well or the video is on an angle that doesn't provide an 'you're almost in the room' experience. Ditto if the quality of the call is not good, it can be a frustrating experience for you and the people you are meeting with, and it can potentially have a negative impact on your credibility.

There are quite a few tips about conferencing and how to maximise your impact – in fact a whole section in this book. This tip is included in this section as the starting place is to have the right technology and evaluate what is right for you. Your laptop likely comes with a built-in camera, microphone and speaker. The question to consider is whether these are of sufficient quality and flexibility to present the best you to your audience.

Here are some tools and equipment to consider:

Webcam

A stand-alone webcam is likely to be better quality than the one built into your laptop. But the main reason for having a separate camera is that you can move it around to get the camera on the best angle to help you be comfortable and create an in-the-room experience. *(And no one needs to see up your nose!)*

Tripod or mount

The best angle for a video conference is exactly the same as for a selfie. This means that the webcam needs to be above eye level and tilted down so that you can look up towards the camera.

Achieving this is going to be a lot easier with a tripod or one of the many varieties of mounts available to use with a webcam – clamps, wall suction, and arm mounts, are just some of the options available.

Microphone

Don't want to sound like you are broadcasting from the bottom of a well? A headset or stand-alone microphone are good options. Using a headset for one-on-one video conferences can be fine. But if you really want to be heard clearly and portray a professional image consider an external microphone. Depending on your audience it may enhance your professionalism if you are not wearing headphones.

Fast internet

Necessity. Not negotiable. Essential. Buffering when you are trying to watch a movie is one thing, but it is just not cool for work. The minimum download and upload speeds that you require do vary based on the service you are using and the type of calls you want to have. For instance, straight video calls, sharing your screen, and group calls all require different minimum download and upload speeds. Given the speed of change to the way we work and the technology we use, the best idea is to get the fastest available that you can afford.

Accounts

You are going to need some type of service, software or application to conduct a video conference. If you work for an organization there is a fair chance that they will have accounts with the service that they prefer you to use.

If not, or you work for yourself, you will need to set up accounts with the services you want to use. There are plenty of free options but even these require you to have an account so that you can access the service. You don't want to be scrambling to set something up if you have a client or prospect who wants to video call you.

If your client has a preferred service that they are comfortable using it can be a good option for you to already have an account set up.

The ability to offer clients a link to contact you (not be dependent on them) will reinforce your credibility as a professional.

Videoconferencing capability is an absolute necessity for your productivity, relationship building and effectiveness. You'll appreciate the time and investment in a professional set-up.

47. Two screens

For Digital Portfolio Manager David Stone, one of the biggest pleasures of working from home is spending time with his two rescue cats. They seem to like it too and like to watch the cursor move around his computer screen *(when they are not snuggled up nearby sleeping)*.

David has set up his home office with fast internet and two monitors, even though he only works from home a couple of days a week. He says, *"It's a better set-up than I have at work!"* Using two monitors can be a great contributor to productivity, and it can reduce the amount of information you print if you are working on two things at the same time.

Whether you want to invest in a second monitor is up to you but here are some of the benefits to consider.

You can reference information while you work

There's no need to print information from one source so that you can refer to it while you are working on another document or application. For instance, you don't need to print a page, type a quote or some numbers from it into an email. With two monitors you can have them side by side. And even better you can copy an item from one document and with the swish of your mouse paste it into another.

Two applications at the same time

You can work on something on one screen and be monitoring your email or social-media feed at the same time. A quick glance to see if your boss has emailed you is more efficient than having to break your concentration to toggle between apps on a single screen. And if you are having a video conference and working with someone on a document you can have your colleague on one screen and the document you are referring to on the other.

Copy and paste

I know I have already mentioned this, but the ease of copy and paste between different documents and programs is an absolute time-saver.

A number of studies *(including ones undertaken or sponsored by organizations that produce monitors)* have shown that users are more productive with dual screens *(fancy that!)*. A study by the University of Utah found that users worked faster and made fewer errors when using dual rather than single monitors.[ii]

You might like working with two monitors so much you consider a third but I'm guessing you're going to need a bigger desk.

48. Security software

This tip is a no-brainer. You need to keep your information secure and your computer in working order. Between viruses, malware, ransomware, hackers, and everything else, the internet can have a lot of drawbacks.

But you can have peace of mind with the appropriate security software. It will perform functions like identifying and removing viruses, detecting and managing spam, and providing backup and firewall services.

If you are on an employer's network there is no doubt a tedious procedure to work through to log on each day. But this humdrum task is facilitating your company keeping their, and your, information secure.

When you are working for yourself it's up to you. Research what you need and make sure you buy, install and use it! I found that setting everything up to run automatically, including auto renewal of my subscriptions, is the best course of action. Set and forget!

Regardless of whether you or your organization is in charge of your security program you can take these added precautions:

- Don't open links or documents that you don't know.
- Protect your passwords and change them often.
- Use strong passwords with letters, capitals, numbers and characters.
- Update your security program when you are prompted.
- Backup your data.
- Be careful when using public Wi-Fi. If you are going to use it, turn off file sharing and don't log into any programs that require a password.
- Lock your devices.

Apply these security precautions to all your devices. It's also important to know where all your devices are at all times to keep your information secure. The strangest place I have found my phone after a frantic search of the house was in my sock drawer, where it didn't come to any harm and I think it was quite comfy. But I was fairly panic-stricken while it was missing.

Take the appropriate precautions, automate your security as much as possible, and just be a little bit suspicious of anything unusual that lands in your inbox. Stay safe!

49. System updates

The most important reason for making sure you keep your system updated regularly is to ensure that you have the most current security settings and are protected from the newest viruses. Plus you'll get all the new features, speed and everything else that those clever developers include in their latest release.

If you work from home all the time, make sure that you have your settings to enable the updates to happen automatically. If you do get prompted for a download – do it! Apparently those evil hackers can turn your auto downloads off, so the best you can do is thwart their efforts and download the update yourself. It may be inconvenient to be interrupted by system housekeeping right when you're trying to get some work done, but it's a lot better than having a vulnerable computer. *(Use the download time as an opportunity to take a break, make a cuppa or call, or go for a walk. Or all three!)*

For those of you who have a computer that is connected to your organization's network and only work from home one or two days a week – make sure that your updates happen at the office. There is a fair chance that they will be quicker on your work network than home, no matter how fast your internet speed. Make sure you do it before your precious work-from-home day when you planned to be super-efficient and get so much done.

Update your systems, people!

50. Tech support

Almost every program or application you use is likely to have some type of support available. This might be as simple as frequently asked questions, online libraries, an online chat service or a help line *(where you get to talk to an actual human being)*.

But there is a chance that at some stage *(it's actually pretty likely)* you will need some kind of in-person human intervention to assist. Installing, fixing and troubleshooting are just some of the types of tech support you might need. Check out what the options are in your area. There may be a local computer-repair store or folks who provide onsite services and will come to you.

Unless you are a techie yourself and have mastery over and above Level 1 support *(close everything down, turn the power off at the wall, wait 10 seconds, and turn it back on again – that's my limit! Do not take this as any form of guidance about what you should do!)* Outsourcing your tech needs is likely to be a good investment, and will allow you to spend your time on the activities that are most important to you.

Tech support will get you up and going, or set-up much faster and with much less frustration. Because when your tech stuff doesn't work – you don't work.

Know how to get the tech support you need.

V. CONFERENCING *(how to maximize your impact)*

Love them or hate them, by phone or by video, with colleagues or clients… conference calls are a frequent reality when you are working from home. Technology enables people to work together regardless of whether they are on the other side of the country or globe. Conference calls facilitate our communication with each other, provide opportunities to engage, and the ability to be effective.

When you work from home they are one of the most important connections to the outside world. They enable you to build rapport with people, participate in a team, meet with clients without leaving home, generate new ideas, ask questions, present, and collaborate. The list goes on.

Even if you only work from home one or two days a week, the ability to attend meetings via a call means that you don't have to change your plans and trudge into the office just because a meeting drops into your diary.

They are, however, somewhat of a double-edged sword. Although they provide the opportunity to engage and participate in work no matter where your customers and colleagues are, it does take some time and thought to set-up and manage these calls so that you can get the most out of them.

These tips are designed to help maximize the impact that you have when you are on conference calls either by video or phone. The more professional you appear, the more credible you are, and the easier it is to communicate with other people.

The physical background you use for a video call, minimizing background noise, closing the door, and getting ready to share your screen are just part of the pre-call preparation. You'll also need to test the technology, dress appropriately, and switch your other devices to silent. And that's all before you even log into a call!

Once you are on a conference call, you need to consider your use of the mute button, how you introduce yourself, and make sure that you have something to say.

It may not seem as easy as jumping on a quick call to have a chat with someone, but once you set yourself up and get in the habit, these tips will make all the difference to how much benefit you get connecting with people by conference calls.

51. Prepare your background (for video calls)

A video conference is one of the best opportunities to promote yourself and build your reputation when you work from home. However, you don't want a video call to detract from the credibility you want to establish, or to look disorganized due to background clutter.

Empty coffee cups? A pile of bills? A whiteboard with confidential information on it? *(I'm just looking around my office now and seeing the types of things I would not want in the background of a video call!)*

Better options include:

- A neat bookcase

- A picture or prints on the wall – big and simple works well

- Some greenery – try a strategically placed indoor plant *(no one will know if it's plastic!)*

Set up your webcam, laptop camera or other device, and check out what the people on the other end of the call are going to see. Then go ahead and decorate your environment *(or just move things out of view of the camera)* so that you are video-ready.

There are also technology solutions that allow you to blur the background or insert backdrops. If you don't have the luxury of a dedicated area you might want to consider these options.

Lighting is also important for the background of your call. Work with any natural light you have, but be careful of windows in the background. What may look like a pretty view to you may, on screen, be glary or cast shadows, making you hard to see. You also don't want a background where people could be wandering by, and also consider what will be in your line of sight. You want to keep eye contact with your caller not be distracted by something else when you are on a call.

Have your background set-up in advance, so that you and what you are saying are the focus of the call. *(There's plenty of room for abandoned coffee cups elsewhere!)*

52. Minimize background noise

Whether you are on a video call, a teleconference, or just a plain old telephone call you want to minimize background noise. If you've got something to say you want to be heard, and you don't want to have to ask people to repeat themselves. Likewise, you don't want any unexpected or irritating distractions interfering with your call.

You may not be able to plan for every contingency, such as the neighbor starting up their lawn mower or leaf blower when you are in the middle of an earnest discussion, but you can do a few things to minimize background noise:

- Let other people in your household know that you are about to make a call (that is, ask them to be quiet!).
- Turn off any sources of noise – music, TV…
- Put your phone on silent.
- Turn off the volume on your laptop so others don't hear your email alerts or another call coming in.
- Make sure your furry friends are happy and not likely to disturb you mid-call.
- Use a good headset so that there is no white noise or echoing. There are headsets available that include noise-cancelling microphones.
- Close doors or windows that might let in outside noise.
- Use the mute button when you are not talking.
- Move to another location.
- Make sure your fan or heating is not generating too much noise – you may want to turn them down or off for the duration of a call.
- Schedule your calls at times you know will be quieter.

And, like most other things in life, there are apps that can help with noise cancellation.

Be conscious of your environment and the noises that could be amplified or unwelcome on a call. Minimizing these background noises will avoid distractions and help make your conference calls as beneficial as possible.

53. Close the door

Closing a door can provide life-saving seconds to escape a fire and, not quite as dramatically, remove the threat of unwanted interruptions while you are on a conference call.

Health and Business Services Advisor Dr. Julie Phillips was on a late-night video conference call from her home office that was doing double duty as a storage area during a kitchen renovation. You can guess what happened… her husband, John, appeared in the background of the call as he needed some pots and pans. He did try and stay out of the picture by crawling across the floor to get to the boxes. Unfortunately, he was still in screen and clearly visible to the other participants on the video. The good thing was that everyone on the call was very good-humored about the interruption. The bonus for Julie was that dinner was ready by the time the call was finished!

If you're fortunate enough to have a dedicated work area with a door – use it. This is important for both video and teleconferences. Sure you might not have a kitchen pantomime playing out in the background but someone walking in on you can be distracting – even on a teleconference. Particularly if you are the one talking at the time of the unwelcome intrusion!

A closed door will also help minimize any background noise from the rest of your home. Let other people at home know that you are just about to jump on a call. If they are not around to tell them, put a sign *(even a sticky note)* on the door to let them know. Or have a prearranged signal – like a closed door!

If you have children who might disregard instructions to leave you alone or are not yet able to read your thoughtfully provided note and you have a lock on the door – consider that as an option!

And if you are storing your kitchen appliances in your office and hoping to have dinner cooked for you, Julie recommends sorting that out as part of your pre-call preparation. Then close the door!

54. Disclose your plans

There's a reason why TV and radio studios use a big, well-lit 'ON AIR' sign when they are broadcasting. To let people know they need to be quiet!

Silence is exactly what you want, too, if you are on a teleconference or a video call. This can be tricky if there are other people at home at the same time. You might have the door of your home office closed and even a stern 'Keep out!' or a mild 'I'm on a call' note stuck to the door, but that will not create a sound barrier to a too-loud TV, blaring music or a happy *(or not happy)* puppy that has positioned itself right outside your door.

Sharing your plans – such as when you have calls and need quiet, what times you're working, and when you are going out – all helps harmony on the home front. And it helps you to take and make calls without interruptions.

If there are other people at home when you have calls to make, let them know what's going on before you get on the call, rather than wildly gesturing for them to shush when you are trying to talk.

Give others an idea of how long you will be on a call, so they can work around you. Provide some advance warning and they may choose to go out! Or to use headphones for their entertainment or phone calls. And they might even be able to help with keeping that noisy puppy out of the way.

55. Prepare to share (your screen)

The ability to share screens is one of the greatest uses of technology for working from home. It can be used to make presentations, conduct training, work through documents with other people, or simply share a document or website that you are referring to. If you can see it on your screen you can share it.

Unfortunately, I have had a number of calls over the years from staff members confessing that they were online chatting during a video conference and their 'private' discussion *(usually about someone else on the call)* had been seen by everybody. Not cool. Apart from being offensive and upsetting to others it also causes a very unnecessary dent to their credibility. It also wasted a considerable amount of their time when they then had to ring all the people on the call to apologize. You don't want to upset others, be embarrassed by what others see on your screen, appear unprofessional or accidentally share confidential information.

Regardless of whether the plan for your call is to share your screen or you decide mid-call that it will be a lot easier to progress a discussion by sharing material here is a short list of things you should do before you share your screen.

Turn off your desktop notifications

Apart from it being completely distracting – there's a good chance you don't want everyone on a conference call to see every email that arrives in your inbox while you are sharing your screen. It can be even worse if you have the display settings for your email show the first couple of lines of text. There might not be any personal information in the emails, but even the subject of an email could be confidential.

Shut down instant messaging

Regardless of whether it's a personal app or an internal company messaging service, you don't want messages appearing while you are sharing your screen. They take up valuable space on your screen, cover the document you are trying to share, and interrupt the flow of the discussion.

I close my instant-messaging apps whenever I am on a conference call or use the Do Not Disturb option even if I am not planning to share my screen. I just don't want the distraction of trying to have a conversation or make a presentation while people are sending me messages at the same time. I find it really annoying when people can see that you are in a meeting but they still send messages. *(I'll get off my soapbox now!)*

Close your windows

I've discussed closing the office windows to minimize background noise, but here I'm talking about all the windows that are open on your device: Facebook, travel sites, email, presentations, the last thing you were reading, confidential material – all of them. Close them before sharing your screen. *(Except what you actually want to share, of course!)*

It is too easy to flick between screens and show something you don't want to share. If they're not open, it can't happen. Close them down!

Open the document you want to share

As part of your pre-call preparation, open the documents you want to share before the call. If it turns out you need another document while you are on a call – stop sharing your screen during the time you are looking for it. Have a little side chat while you are setting up, rather than let your colleagues or clients see the titles of all your documents and files.

And when you've finished your call don't forget to turn the screen sharing off. You don't want to undo all your good work.

Preparation of all kinds is important for effective calls and contributes to your positive reputation. Preparing to share your screen is one more pixel of the picture.

56. Test the technology

Even if you've used it 100 times before it is always a good idea to test your technology before a call. Okay I'll give you some leeway… if it's a simple dial-in that you use every week and you know exactly what you are doing, fair enough.

But if you are doing anything different, with any different technology or from a different location, test the technology so that you know it works. Delays while you try and work out how to do something mid-call or if you can't be heard or seen, or are unable to open something or connect to something else, all take away from the professionalism of a call, waste your and other people's time, and are lost opportunities for a meeting to be effective.

Testing your technology might be as simple as checking you have cell signal or internet access, or that you have the correct log-in details ready and that links are working.

More comprehensive testing and even a rehearsal might be warranted if you are going to be:

- hosting the call
- presenting
- using a new app
- sharing your screen
- asking for questions
- managing chats or collaboration with participants, or
- anything else that is a bit tricky or you haven't done before.

Test the technology so that things go smoothly.

57. Dress appropriately

Hair combed; make-up or a shave; proper clothes. As tiresome as these might be when you work from home they are absolutely necessary for video calls. Dressing appropriately sets the tone and reinforces the impression that you are professional, credible, and actually working *(all of which you are!)*.

Presenting yourself appropriately by video is also respectful to the people you are talking to – clients, staff, your boss, and other contacts. And it can make a big difference to help you get into work mode and present or speak confidently.

This doesn't mean that you have to sit around the house in your best suit waiting in case someone contacts you by video; although you do probably want to be presentable *(at least from the waist up)*. But it does mean that you need to be appropriately dressed when you have a video call planned. At the very least be prepared in case you have an unexpected request. A shirt ironed and ready to grab can save a lot of angst when a meeting invite for a teleconference in the next few minutes pops into your inbox.

If you are working in your activewear and someone rings you unannounced by video and you don't feel appropriately dressed don't answer the call. Ring them back *(no video!)* or change into your emergency outfit, brush your hair, clean your teeth – whatever you feel you need to present yourself appropriately, then video call them back.

What is appropriate will be different depending on what you do and the people you are working with. It can be a very personal decision about how you need to dress to feel confident to present yourself at your best.

A good rule of thumb is to wear whatever is expected for your industry or company. This could range from traditional office wear or formal workwear, to business casual, smart-casual or very casual – depending on your business.

Think of it this way… What you would wear to go and visit a client? That's what you should wear for a video call with a client. Whatever the expected dress standard is in your office is the appropriate way to be dressed to interact with your colleagues online. And so on.

And do remember that if you are only fancy from the waist up, don't stand up mid-call! We've all heard horror stories about video calls that went horribly wrong when someone moved during a call to grab a file or answer the door and revealed more than they intended. Credibility disappears along with any pants that are not present. *(It's hard to believe but a survey of 800 Americans revealed that 1 in 10 didn't put on underwear, pants or bras for a video call.[i])*

Now that I've planted that image in your brain and you're worrying about what your last video caller was wearing *(sorry about that)*, just remember why you are using video. Usually it is to build a closer connection with someone or facilitate relationships within a team.

Video calls can help reinforce your capability and enhance your professionalism. I have been known to apply lip gloss before a teleconference just to get into work mode. It's ridiculous and pointless from the perspective of the call, but it reinforces for me that I am not just in my own home environment; I am 'at work'. *(It's also a good way to use up all the colors I don't like anymore and it helps with dry lips!)*

Dress appropriately for video calls regardless of the fact that you are working from home. And enjoy the freedom of casual gear on the days that are video-free *(even if you need some lip gloss!).*

58. Get yourself ready

It goes without saying *(I hope)* that you need to prepare for a conference call. Have to hand any documents you need to present, notes or reminders about what you want to say *(discreetly placed at the side of your camera if it's a video call)*, actions to report on, or research on the topic being discussed.

And you also need to have the technology sorted, noisy puppy/bird happily occupied elsewhere, windows shut to block out any neighbors who decide to mow the lawn just as you are about to speak, and let anyone else at home know that they need to be as quiet as mice so you can have a professional call. But wait there's more…

Take a bathroom break

Former British Prime Minister David Cameron received worldwide news headlines for his use of the full-bladder technique, apparently in aid of honing his concentration, during international negotiations. Being *'desperate for a pee'*, as was widely quoted at the time, may or may not have achieved better outcomes. And it was certainly not supported by the many experts who commented on the negative health aspects of his revelation.

Personally, I think it's a whole lot more comfortable if you have been to the bathroom prior to a call. Some meetings are long. Very long. Too long. *(But that's another topic!)* If you do 'have to go' during a meeting, politely excuse yourself and go. Everybody pees.

But, DO NOT take your phone to the bathroom under any circumstances! I do not care how competent you think you are at using the mute button. Don't do it.

Grab a glass of water

Apart from the health benefits, a glass of water on standby to sip during a meeting can create a pause to give you some time to think about what you are going to say. Or help with that nervous tickle in your throat. If it's going to be a long meeting, you might need a jug!

Beverages

Time making a coffee or tea before a meeting will not only result in you having a coffee or tea for your meeting *(win)*, it's a chance to stand up and walk away from your desk for a few minutes. It gives you time to mentally close off whatever else you were working on so that you are ready and focused on the next meeting.

Sipping on a coffee or other beverage of choice can help you relax and feel prepared as you join your meeting. And it gives you something to do when you follow the next tip and log into your call early.

Log into your call early

It doesn't seem to matter how many times you've used an app before or know the dial-in numbers of a teleconference off by heart, if you don't start logging in before the scheduled time of the meeting you are going to be late.

Dial in two to three minutes early and you will be on time and ready to be awesome. And have time to enjoy your coffee while it is still nice and hot.

Preparing yourself for a conference call is just as important as preparing your content. The time spent will help you perform at your best.

59. Switch to silent

Our devices ting, ding, and ring to let us know a message has arrived, we need to be somewhere, or someone wants to talk with us. Handy little reminders. But incredibly distracting for you and others if you're making a presentation and your phone starts ringing. Or you're on the phone and there are all sorts of alerts coming from your laptop.

Avoid these distractions by putting all of your devices on silent *before* you log into a conference call. If you're using your phone, make sure any messaging apps and alerts on your computer are muted and any other phones you may have are on silent. Ditto if you are on a call via your laptop – make sure any phones and other devices are set to silent.

I'm also inclined to turn off the 'vibrate on silent setting' as well. Not so much because other people on a call will hear it, but because I get distracted. If I am presenting or even talking, an alert of any kind can make me lose my train of thought.

Don't forget to turn them back on when you have finished your call as it is terribly inconvenient when you leave the phone somewhere on your wanders through the house and you can't call yourself to find it. I can confirm that I have wasted a lot of time looking for my phone when it was left on silent. Particularly the day it *(eventually)* turned up in my sock drawer.

Switch your devices to silent before a conference call, so that they do not become distractions for yourself and others.

60. Use your mute button

Hands up if you've ever multi-tasked on a conference call? Churned out a few emails perhaps? Had an online chat with someone? Written your presentation for your next meeting? We know that we should be paying 100% attention to the call, but that keyboard is just oh-so-tempting when there is an agenda item that isn't relevant to us.

The click, click, click of you typing away is likely to give away that you aren't completely engaged, and it can potentially distract the speaker or other attendees at the meeting. Now I am not advocating that you should or shouldn't be multi-tasking *(no judgment here)*, but if you use your mute button you can avoid giving yourself away with loud tappity, tap, tap sounds.

Apparently people get up to all sorts of things during teleconferences. In one survey, 82% of people said they work on unrelated items while they are on a call.[ii] *(I do wonder about the honesty of the other 18 %.)* What is more surprising is some of the things they admitted to doing while on a call. I get that 65% were doing other work and 63% said they send emails *(I am guilty of both)*... but the 47% who go to the restroom? 25% who play video games? And 9% who exercise during conference calls? Why on earth are they on the call in the first place? Whatever you are doing, the mute button will avoid introducing noise from your other activity into the meeting.

It's good practice to let people know you are putting yourself on mute while you wait for a meeting to start. They'll understand why there might be a short delay while you get yourself off mute when it is time for you to say something. And they'll know that it is not you who is responsible for any distracting background noises.

Don't under any circumstances take your phone to the bathroom, even if it is on mute. One accidental press of that helpful button and you'll be sharing way too much!

But for anything else, make it standard practice to use your mute button. It's there for a reason.

61. Sit up straight

Conference calls are an opportunity to connect with your customers, colleagues and others in a way that builds rapport that is unlikely to be possible by email alone. *(No matter how many cute emojis you include ☺)*

They provide the chance to showcase your abilities and contributions to your boss, colleagues or to a client. An impressive presentation, an insightful question, and demonstrating your understanding of a situation can all contribute to your credibility. Which is important, regardless of whether you work from home or elsewhere, in order to achieve your work objectives and career goals.

Making a positive contribution in meetings is crucial to achieving your objectives. When you work at home and conference calls are your principal means of communication, the nuance of body language and tone of voice become even more important than when you are in a meeting face to face.

Here are some things to consider doing during video conferences:

- Sit up straight – it helps to better project your voice.

- Control your facial expressions – a picture tells a story, so no eye rolling or pulling faces. Maintain facial expressions as if you were in the room.

- Try and be as natural as possible. Don't touch or cover your face because you are nervous about how you look on screen – it can be very distracting for others.

- Make eye contact with people.

- Use your hands as you would in person; gesture if you like to talk with your hands, hold a pen or rest them on the desk. Crossed arms will look just as closed off to an idea on a video call as it does in an in-person meeting. Other people on the call won't know that you are just cold!

Even if you are on a teleconference, being aware of how you sit is also important to help you project your voice so that it is easier for other participants on the call to hear you. Modulating your voice and being conscious not to talk too fast will also help people understand what you are saying. It also leaves space for people to be able to ask questions.

Sit up straight and use your body language and voice to make conference calls a valuable tool to help you project the best you.

62. Introduce yourself

When you are at a face-to-face meeting, the etiquette is to greet the people you know and introduce yourself to anyone you don't know. This introduction helps you find out exactly who the person is and hopefully provide some clues about why they are in the meeting, which should make the discussion much more effective.

Likewise when you are on a conference call, introducing yourself is the polite thing to do. It makes others feel comfortable, and it shows that you are there and ready to contribute to a successful meeting.

If you are on a video conference you'll be able to see who you know and who you don't. Say hello to those you do and introduce yourself to those you don't. If you are not running the conference make an opportunity at the start of the call to let the person who is leading the call know that you don't know everyone and ask if you could make some quick introductions.

On a teleconference announce yourself as an attendee at the beginning of the call and each time you speak during the call say who you are. Unless you are on a call with very few participants you don't want to have to rely on how good others are at recognizing your voice. You never know how good other people's voice-recognition software is! Such a shame if you make a brilliant contribution and no one knows it's you! A simple *"It's Karen here..."* is all it takes for me to let people know who is speaking *(please feel free to use your own name!)*. If others are speaking and you don't know who it is and you want to ask them a question or build on the point they just made, it is perfectly acceptable to ask who was speaking, or if the person was who you thought it was.

Introductions are necessary and good professional etiquette for conference calls.

63. Have something to say

If you are attending a meeting for goodness' sake… have something to say!

If you are taking the time to attend a meeting, it should be because you have something to contribute and some reason for being there. If you don't, then don't go. *(Unless you are going to get fired, of course, and then you'd need to think about why you have a job that has meetings that waste your time. But that's a topic for another book!)*

True, there are meetings when you attend to learn new information, but even these forums usually have the opportunity to ask questions at the end. If you attend a meeting, it's important to have something to say – even if it is just to ask a thoughtful question. Meetings are a unique opportunity to demonstrate your capability, while you build your credibility and reputation – even more so when you are working from home and meetings are full conference calls. It's absolutely vital to say something if everyone else is in a room and you are the only one hanging off the end of a phone. You can be in genuine danger of people forgetting that you are even at the meeting.

Obviously you don't just speak up to hear the sound of your own voice; it has to be worthwhile. An insightful question can remind people you're on the call, demonstrate that you understand the issue, and you might even learn something from the answer! You can also share insights or get involved in a brainstorming discussion.

Agreeing with or summarizing what has been discussed also demonstrates that you are engaged and understood the topic under discussion. People love hearing their ideas repeated, and they'll tend to agree with everything you say! *"Can I confirm that we have agreed to…?"*, *"Do you mean…?"* or *"Are you saying that…?"* are some simple ways of getting involved in and letting people know you understood a discussion. They agree, you demonstrate you've been listening, and your presenter is happy because they know they were understood. Win, win, win!

Having something to say and contributing to conference calls helps make the best use of your and everybody else's time.

VI. KEEP IN TOUCH *(how to stay top of mind)*

Keeping in touch ensures that you stay 'top of mind' with time-poor managers and clients who must make decisions in a hurry and when they are under pressure. For your career to develop, your client list to grow and simply to have equal opportunity to be successful in your work with office-based associates (who may have greater access to people and information), it's essential that you are visible.

Staying in contact with colleagues, clients, and your network helps them remember you when it comes to new opportunities. It can even keep you informed about things you need to know to do your job. Staying top of mind will help you receive acknowledgment for your achievements, and build your profile and reputation to assist your business and career objectives.

If others know about you, what you do and what you are capable of, there's more chance that you'll be on their radar when decisions are being made about resources, promotions, bonuses or new business.

Your reputation is your most valuable career asset. To build it up, you need to remind others *(or in fact let them know)* that you exist.

So how do you step out from behind your excellent work to build your profile and become top of mind? Some ideas include being available, checking in regularly, and staying in touch with your manager. You can also use video to stay in touch so people can see your smiling face, pick up the phone to call, and take time to build rapport. In addition, you can go to the office (sometimes), share your achievements, connect with people, and get involved – initiatives that will help build all-important relationships.

Keep in touch with people and stay top of mind – all from the comfort of your own home!

64. Be available

Working from home may be more accepted than previously, but there is still the perception in some quarters that you are 'at home' rather than 'at work' even though, you know, you are in full work mode. One work-from-homer told me that she finds it very frustrating when workmates contact her about a work matter and say, *"Oh, sorry to annoy you at home!"* This is despite sending regular emails to her team to let them know where she is on the one to two days a week that she works from home.

To be effective, whether you work for an organization or are running your own show, it helps people stay in contact with you if they know when you are available. The flexibility of working from home, as we know, is brilliant. But if every time someone calls you the background noise suggests that you are out and about or they just can't get hold of you then people stop trying.

David Stone, who works from home a couple of days a week for a major telecommunications organization, does so on set days of the week. His team know where he is and how to contact him, and when he is working from home he is contactable by phone, chat app or video.

There are a few simple things to help you be available to other people:

- Schedule regular catch-ups so that people know they have time with you.
- Make sure your calendar is up-to-date so that your availability is visible in internal company calendars.
- Let people know the best times of day to call for check-ins, or the best way to get in contact with you for urgent issues.

As tempting as it is when you are busy, avoid blocking out your diary or setting your availability to 'Do not disturb' too often. If the people you are working with can't get you regularly they will start ignoring these barriers and contact you regardless. The precious times you do need to be undisturbed for work or your breaks may no longer be respected.

To stay connected and work with your contacts, colleagues, manager and/or clients be available to them. It will help your ability to work and communicate with them, and ultimately help you to be more effective in your work.

65. Check in

'Out of sight, out of mind' goes the old saying. Even though teams and businesses are often dispersed, when you work from home you risk missing out on knowing what is going on in the office and being able to let people know about your contributions.

It's in your interest to invest a little time to 'check-in' with people and remind them that you are around. This can make the difference to others remembering to tell you about things, including you in meetings, and identifying opportunities of work you could or should be involved in. When you work for yourself these regular 'check-ins' remind clients about the value you are adding to their business and may even prompt them to give you more work!

It is much better to reach out to others rather than thinking you will be 'top of mind' to your super-busy colleagues and clients.

There is no shortage of technology to help you do this, ranging from phone calls, texts, emails, online chats… the list goes on. In one role, I would simply text a smiley emoji each morning to the managers who were reporting to me. It let them know that I was on deck and working and when I got their smiley response I knew that they had started work and it was okay to contact them. It started with just smiley faces, but after a few months we got quite creative with our use of emojis to tell little stories – which was a fun way to start the day.

Use the many tools that are available to check in, and be top of mind for opportunities and information.

66. Use video

As tiresome as it is to have to dress appropriately, test the technology, and look at yourself on the screen (especially if you hate it!), using video and letting people see you is an effective tool to stay in touch and make your communications more effective.

Video calls provide the opportunity to build rapport and develop relationships with colleagues and clients. It is better than a phone call and exceedingly superior to a text or online chat if there is any detailed information that you want to discuss.

A video chat or conference lets your colleagues and customers engage with you in a more meaningful way. The impression you make through your appearance, eye contact, and the body language you use will all complement what you are saying.

It also provides a little more leeway for social chitchat and getting to know the other person. This helps build relationships, which is particularly important when you are remote from the people you work with.

Rather than opting for a teleconference, suggest to colleagues that you use video. Ask your manager or clients if they are okay with using video for your regular meetings. Even for one-on-one calls include in the meeting invite that you send that it is a video call; that way you won't catch people out in their activewear! It can be a very awkward start if you make a video call and the other person wasn't expecting you to contact them that way.

Video is a powerful tool to keep in touch – when people think of you they will recall an image of you, not picture themselves talking to you through a phone.

The professional image you can portray, the depth of relationship you can build and the added effectiveness of what you communicate through video will all help you stay front of mind with the people who matter.

67. Stay in contact with your manager/client

If you work for a company, your manager is the person who impacts the projects you are allocated to work on, who you are asked to work with, sets your targets, assesses your performance, provides coaching and feedback, is responsible for your salary review, and can influence your reputation *(good or bad)* through the opinions they share about you. *(We're talking about what they are meant to do here, not necessarily what they do.)*

These are all important reasons to stay in contact with your manager, so that you can seek their feedback, keep them across what you are working on, and let them know about your achievements.

When you work for yourself, it is your client who, effectively, is your manager. The relationship is different, of course, but they also determine the work you get, what you get paid, and your professional reputation.

Regardless of whether we are talking about a manager or a client the goals are similar: for them to value and support you and your work.

Staying in contact with your manager or client will help you achieve your objectives as they get to know you and appreciate your contributions.

Here are some ideas to make this communication effective:

Understand how they like to communicate

Text, calls, or emails? People often have different preferences about how they like to communicate for different topics. It's likely they'll want to hear from you in different ways based on whether you are managing an imminent disaster, a customer complaint is brewing, or you are having a regular catch-up.

The best way to know how they like to communicate is to ask them. *(I know: revolutionary idea!)* If you know what information they want, when and how they would like to receive it, it is likely to make the communication much more effective and efficient.

Likewise, if you understand how they work and the rhythm of their working day it will make it much easier for you to 'catch them' for a quick chat when you have something you want to talk about outside of any regularly scheduled meetings.

Ask questions

Asking questions, and listening to the answers, is often the cornerstone of any good communication. It's especially important when you are not working in the same office and can't see the comings and goings, the body language, and the pressures that the people you are working with might be grappling with.

A good first question when you contact someone is to ask if it's a good time to talk or when they would be available to have a chat. Just because they answer your call doesn't mean that they have time for a deep discussion. Unless the matter is urgent, you won't have a meaningful conversation with someone if they are preoccupied with another emergency or commitment.

Here are some other things to ask that may help your relationship with your manager and/or clients:

- What their goals and priorities are
- Exactly what they want you to achieve
- When things are due
- How they want to receive updates from you
- Anything else you can help with
- What else is going on
- How they are *(managers and clients are people, too!)*

Clear expectations about how and when you communicate are important to a positive and constructive relationship with your manager or clients.

Meeting those expectations and keeping the lines of communication open will enhance your credibility and provide you with the means to engage with them so that they value and support you and your work.

If you don't have good communication with them it's pretty hard to build good rapport for them to, in return, get to know how you are. Stay in touch and stay front of mind.

68. Take time to build rapport

Whether it's a personal connection due to a shared interest, or the way you like to work together, having a good rapport makes it so much easier to work with other people. The definition of rapport is as simple as an 'understanding between people', according to thesaurus.com.

Among the many benefits of having a good rapport with colleagues or clients are an increased level of trust in your work, a greater likelihood of sharing information with you, and a higher chance that they will recommend you and your ideas to others. Not to mention that it usually makes the experience of working much more enjoyable!

But it doesn't just happen. Building rapport means investing some time in the relationship in order to develop an understanding with others.

Here are some approaches that can help, particularly when you are working remotely:

Use people's names

Using someone's name is a sign that you have at least taken enough interest in them to remember their name. Dale Carnegie, author of the 1936 self-help book "How to Win Friends and Influence People" said *"A person's name is, to that person, the sweetest and most important sound in any language."* It's an old book, but I re-read it every couple of years because the tips are good, and I think he is very respectful about being genuine with people, not trying to trick them into liking you. This is not what you are trying to do! *(And I think he was onto something as apparently the book has sold more than 15 million copies... something I can only dream about!)*

You don't have to go over the top, but at least use names when you say hello or goodbye, and the effort will be appreciated. People will remember that you remembered them.

Match their communication style

If you are working with people who dive in and get straight to the point, they will appreciate it if you do this, too. Body language, pace of speaking, and the type of language they use are all opportunities to match the communication style of others.

The advantage of doing this is that it is easier for them and can help reinforce that you are on the same wavelength, whereas a style different to their own, might be a distraction for them.

This applies to written communications as well, such as the style of introduction; how they sign off, and how they like to see information presented in emails. Long rambling prose does not work so well with people who like to use bullet points. If they sign off with their initials they are likely to find a formal sign-off a bit jarring.

You can even match your communication style in text messages. If they send you messages laced with emojis they are likely to be highly visual and use graphics to help express what they want to say. Responding to them in the same way is a good way to effectively communicate and build rapport at the same time.

Demonstrate that you are listening

People appreciate being listened to. Asking questions or clarifying a point based on what you have been told is a superb technique to demonstrate that you have been listening. Body language, such as eye contact *(for video calls obviously)* can also reinforce that you are paying attention. And some people like to see *(again, for video)* that you are taking notes.

You can also use the notetaking technique on teleconferences and phone calls. A quick explanation of why you paused before speaking again – *'I was just capturing that last point'* – will demonstrate that you are listening quite nicely.

Ask questions

There is nothing like genuine interest in people or their work to help build rapport. Asking questions will help you learn information, demonstrate that you have understood what has been said, clarify your understanding and solve problems. *(There are more, but I do want to finish this book eventually!)*

The point is, asking questions is an incredibly powerful communication technique. It will help you build rapport and your credibility with others.

Use interest-creating remarks

I learnt about interest-creating remarks in my sales-skills training *(back in the day)*. A comment that you have noticed something significant about their business – for instance, reference to a recent achievement – as you are starting a call demonstrates that you are interested and a little bit knowledgeable about them. Asking a question about their current priorities also works, too!

It is an effective technique in any conversation when you want to build rapport. *(Which I would suggest is every conversation.)* It can be a platform for more questions and further discussion or it can be simply acknowledged before you get down to business. Either way it demonstrates your knowledge and interest in them and what they do.

Take some time for chitchat

It might be at the beginning or the end of a conversation, but a little time spent on chitchat can be a good investment of your time. A short side conversation about a shared interest, the weather or other work topics can help you get to know someone a little better and for them to know you. It's a good start to building rapport with the people you are working with.

69. Call

If I had a dollar for every time I heard my former colleague and long-time senior executive in sales, Steven McDonald, say to one of his team, *"Just pick up the phone and talk to them,"* I wouldn't be working from home or anywhere. I wouldn't need to. I would have a lot of dollars. Steven said he has often seen his team email back and forth to each other and to people elsewhere in the business, and generally just wait for a response. From experience, he knows that calling cuts through delays and brings your issue to the top of the list.

As convenient as email, text and messaging services are (and in some circumstances they do have an advantage), there is nothing that replaces actually talking to another human being. Whether it's to short-circuit issues, find out information, or build rapport, talking to people is one of the most powerful forms of communication.

It might take a little longer to get hold of someone or work your way through the social niceties of asking them how they are – but a call gives you the opportunity to provide context, ask questions, and have a real-time two-way communication.

It can be faster, too. I often explain when I ring someone that I thought it would be quicker to give them a quick call rather than send an email because I can speak faster than I can type. With the average conversation rate in English being 120–150 words per minute and a typical average typing speed of 40 words per minute, it takes a lot of extra chitchat to take up more time talking than typing. Once others get over the shock that you've rung and not sent yet another email to get lost in their inbox they usually seem to appreciate the ability to work through issues with you.

Talking to people helps you stay front of mind with colleagues and clients, and it gives you some actual human contact while you are working.

Pick up the phone and call people!

70. Go to the office (sometimes)

This is a tip for those who work from home (café, park or any other place you choose) full-time. Even if you only take a day or two a week away from the office for the productivity and flexibility you gain working from home – you know there are *some* benefits to being in the office.

Face-to-face meetings, the social chitchat, the elevator conversations with people you don't talk to often, and just generally being seen, all help keep you front of mind, in touch with what is going on in the business, and considered when it comes to the assignment of projects, inclusion in activities, promotions and other career opportunities.

This is out of the question if you live a really long distance from your office or customer, but if it's viable for you to 'pop-in' for an odd day when there's an important meeting or you want to collaborate on a project with someone – going to the office can be extremely worthwhile.

Just your presence can remind people that you're part of the team and contributing to the business. Combine this with a couple of effective meetings, a coffee catch-up, and a working lunch for a day well spent.

Not only that, it's a nice break from the routine of being at home. Spending time with your co-workers or clients can also stimulate your ideas and give you insights that will benefit your work. It can also make you appreciate, even more, that you don't have to wrestle with the commute each day and the flexibility that you have (*says she, typing in her gym outfit about to squeeze in a quick cardio session when office-based workers are still battling the late-afternoon traffic*).

Going to the office, sometimes, will help you stay in touch, assist your work, and keep you top of mind with colleagues, the boss or clients.

71. Share your wins

"My results speak for themselves" and *"My good work will be noticed"* say optimistic work-from-homers. Maybe. Maybe not. You can leave it to chance and hope that your contributions are noticed, or you can actively manage your reputation.

Managers often work in stressful situations and to tight deadlines that don't allow them the time to fully review your contributions, or think about whether you are the best person for a new opportunity. When you work from home, out-of-sight can literally mean out-of-mind. Give your manager or clients a helping hand so that they will think of you often. Don't hide in the background; make it easy for the people who can impact your working life to think of you by making your accomplishments known.

The reality is that those who make decisions, potentially about your future, need to know who has the knowledge, skills, and attitude to do what is required – who will help them and the business be successful. It's not just about who gets promoted, but who gets nominated to work on high-profile projects or attend training or meetings with senior stakeholders. For small businesses and consultants it's about who gets given the work.

If they don't know your capabilities, the experience you have and the results you have achieved, they can't possibly know that you're the right person for an opportunity. And they may not realize that you are the right person they need when they are sitting in the office considering their options. If they know your achievements, it can help make you top of mind.

Here are some ways you can share your wins:

- Send your manager or client a weekly report with key achievements *(concise bullet points are recommended!)*.

- If something great happens related to what you are working on, send them an email or text or give them a call straightaway… people always love to be the first to hear good news.

- Mention them in team meetings.
- Add key achievements to your LinkedIn profile.
- Volunteer to help a colleague based on your successful experience.
- Subtly drop achievements into conversations *(the elevator pitch for those days when you do go to the office)*.

One of the most important aspects of sharing your wins is to give credit to other people who helped you achieve them. Teamwork and stakeholder engagement are key skills, and acknowledging the contributions of others will demonstrate your abilities in this area and be appreciated by those you recognize.

Share your wins and you will also be sharing your value, capability and potential; which will help you positively impact your reputation.

72. Connect

When you work from home you may not be able to connect with colleagues in the office kitchen for a chat about the work that you are doing or the meeting that just finished. Casual work encounters are a bit trickier when you have to make an effort to leave home to make them happen.

Yet connections with other people are important. They provide you with social interactions, ideas, information, and broaden your outlook. When you work from home it is so easy to get focused on the work you are doing and not be aware of what else is happening out in the big, wide business world. I'm not talking about your regular checks of Facebook, Instagram, Twitter or any other type of social media you have. Business connections are necessary to keep you across information that is relevant to your job, expose you to new skills, and alert you to possibilities and opportunities.

Attending networking events is important but not always possible. But wherever you are located there is a worldwide business network available online. One of the biggest of these is LinkedIn. Until something new comes along, it really is *the* platform for business connections – not just a place to hang out if you are looking for a new job. There are also numerous forums for specific industries, geographies and professions.

Connecting with people on platforms such as LinkedIn means you don't need to keep track of their email address and you have an easy way to keep in touch. You can see what they post and share and what their business interests are. And they can get to know you in the same way.

A few quick things to remember about connecting and being connected online:

- Always personalize an invitation with a reminder of where you met or why you would like to connect.

- Send an invitation soon after you meet people, whether physically or virtually, as your connection will seem the most relevant to them at the time.

- Make sure that your profile information and picture is up-to-date.

- Reach out and stay in contact with your connections.

- Participate in groups, make appropriate comments on posts, and share business-related content that reflects your interests and the image you want to convey.

LinkedIn, other business forums, or your company's internal social media platform are not the places to share photos from your weekend, or of your pets or what you're having for dinner.

Connecting with people in these forums can build and enhance your credibility and your professional reputation. Be professional, be authentic, and be generous with your recognition of others and your knowledge.

You never know: your next client or your next job might be influenced by one of these people.

Connect with people to keep in touch and be top of mind.

73. Get involved in activities

If you work for an organization there's a good chance that you are on at least one distribution list, which means you get invited to the morning teas, bake sales, and myriad other social-club activities that you can't possibly attend. You work at home, right? When you live an hour's commute away or in another state, it's not so easy to pop in to these events and get to know your fellow workers. When you are remote from clients or customers there is no ability for you to join them when they head to the kitchen for a social activity.

Apart from the aforementioned brownies, these social activities do serve another purpose *(and I do not mean to underestimate the importance of the brownie or other snacks!)*. Social catch-ups can break down silos between departments, allow people to discover shared interests, build relationships and unite people with a shared purpose or support of a common cause – such as a charity or social-responsibility initiative. Not to mention that it's a good chance to increase your visibility, just simply by being there.

Even though you may not be able to participate in the office-based social activities there are still plenty of ways you can be involved in activities that will help you keep in touch and gain some of the benefits of these extracurricular activities. You could:

- Share the fundraising activities of your colleagues with your network.

- Contribute to a newsletter.

- Join a committee.

- Volunteer for a project outside your job description.

- Mentor a colleague or contact.

- Scan a handwritten note to be printed out and included in a special-occasion/farewell card.

- Participate in a competition such as a fantasy football league *(or start one up!)*.

You don't have to work for an organization to get involved with others. If you are running your own show you can participate in out-of-work activities with your clients, groups that you are a member of, and people in your network.

Not only will these kinds of activities help keep you in touch, they can also provide you with social interactions and just make work more enjoyable. And that is something we all need to keep top of mind!

VII. CAREER DEVELOPMENT *(how to choose your future)*

Ongoing career development is important so that you have choices for your future. Choices about where you work, who you work for, and the kind of work you do.

Networking, working with a mentor, and ongoing learning all contribute to the skills, knowledge and experience you need to perform well in your current role and be ready for your next one. Some of the reasons you may choose to care about your career development include:

You need to eat!

Along with those other basics of life – shelter, clothing and Wi-Fi – food is right up there on the list of things you need to pay for. Having the skills to advance your career and the opportunities to communicate the value that you contribute impacts your options and ensures that you have the ability to negotiate what you're paid. If you're going to spend your time working, shouldn't you earn as much as you can? And eat as well as you want? And be able to afford unlimited Wi-Fi?

The minutes tick by slowly

If you don't enjoy your work, nothing feels slower than the minutes counting down to knock-off time – even if you are only looking to escape to the next room at home. And there are plenty of them in your working life… *minutes, that is!* In fact, 4,920,960 is a reasonably conservative estimate of the number of minutes you will be working during your career. *(For the number crunchers, that's 8 hours a day, 233 days of the year for 44 years… it's actually 295,257,600 seconds, but I didn't want to freak you out…)*

It's a lot of time to spend watching the clock if you're not doing something you at least like.

The person most interested in your career is… you!

That's right. The person who looks back at you in the mirror every morning is the one who has the most to win or lose from your career decisions. They are the one who is in the position to make the biggest difference to your career.

They are also the only person who is going to be with you your entire career – and who has the most interest in what you do and how you do it.

Other people may be supportive and provide you with coaching, guidance and training. They may provide you with unbelievable opportunities, great advice or fabulous sponsorship. But you are going to be with you your whole life. The choices you make are up to you. *Be nice to that joker in the mirror, and focus on your career as well as your work.*

Being good at what you do is not enough

You do need to be good at your job. In fact, you need to be the very best at your job that you can. But that is unlikely to be enough in the madcap world of business targets, customer demands, and busy schedules. Nor is being dedicated, working long hours or leaping over small buildings in a single bound!

You need the skills to communicate who you are, what you do, and the contributions that you make. You need to be able to sell your ideas for others to understand your contributions and appreciate the value that you bring to your role.

You need the skills to be effective in your work, to build a professional reputation, and to proactively manage your career so that you are able to make the best choices and negotiate the best outcomes for you.

Focus on your career development *so that you can do what you like, earn what you're worth, and have options for your future.*

74. Set goals

If you don't know where you are going it's pretty hard to work out how to get there. Finding your way around a shopping mall, traveling across town, and working on your career – they all have one thing in common. You need to know where you are trying to get to so that you head off in the right direction.

I'd argue that even if you want to be doing exactly the job you are doing now, for a long time, you still need to set that as a goal. Developing your skills to cope with new technology, keeping up with current trends, and developing contacts are all necessary just to maintain the status quo.

Setting career goals also contributes to job satisfaction in your current role. When you understand how what you are doing now fits into your long-term plan it can make your efforts feel more worthwhile.

Career goals are important to allow you to plan for career progression and to have confidence that when things change with your work *(which they will)* you will have the knowledge, skills and experience to secure your next opportunity.

And it is a matter of *when* things change, because they will. Even when you have a job you love, people change, customer requirements change, company priorities change, technology changes, and work changes. When you have your own business, clients change, projects finish, and demand for your services can ebb and flow.

When you set career or business goals you have clarity about what you are working towards. This can have a huge bearing on many of the day-to-day decisions you make about how to spend your time, who to connect with, and the projects or customers you take on.

When you set your goals, here are some ideas to consider:

Where you are now?

Take an inventory of where you are now and ask yourself: What skills do I have? How deep is my level of industry knowledge or subject-area expertise? What experience and capabilities have I got?

What you are good at?

Write a list of the things that you regularly receive positive feedback about and the tasks that you know you are good at. You don't have to be modest; it's your list, you're not going to post it anywhere, and nobody else is going to be making comments... unless you choose to share it with a mentor or trusted advisor for feedback. Be brutally honest with yourself about how good you are.

What do you like to do?

Go back to the list of all the things you are good at and cross off the things you really don't like to do. Just because you are good at something, doesn't mean you like it. You may not be able to totally abolish everything you don't like from a job you want, but you don't have to make a goal for something you really don't like doing.

How do you like to work?

Do you like to work with people or on your own? Don't assume just because you work from home that the answer is on your own. Think about how you spend your day and you may find that the best bits are when you are working virtually with others.

Do you like to work in a role where you have lots of autonomy or specific direction? Do you prefer sitting behind a desk or being out and about? Do you spend your day thinking and problem solving or getting stuff done *(or both)*? This understanding can help when you are making decisions about what you want for *your* future.

How do you make decisions that are good for you?

Think through how you have made important decisions in the past that worked out well for you. How did you decide what subjects to take at school? Or which university course to enrol in? How did you decide to move house, move city, or which job to take?

When you have an understanding of how you have made successful decisions in the past, it can give you some ideas about how to make decisions about your career goals, for now and the future.

What do you want to do?

Now that is the $64 million question. Make your goals what you really want to do, achieve, realize or experience. It may or may not involve working from home, but just because that's how you work now doesn't mean that you cannot have and be working toward goals that are different from how you work today.

Set your goals, and you are on the way to developing the career you want for your future.

75. Have a plan

Developing a career or business plan will help you think through the actions you need to take in order to achieve your goals.

You may have had a plan previously that worked or, despite your best intentions and well-formulated goals, went off track. Whether your plan includes attending network events, devoting time to developing your skills, or any other type of activity, sometimes other things take precedence. People get sick, there are urgent deadlines, demanding clients, unplanned activities, house guests... all sorts of things can get in the way of your plans to do more to develop your career and work towards your goals. When you work from home, with all of the things that can be going on around you *and* the pressures of work, keeping focused on your career development can seem like a luxury.

But developing a career plan does not have to be onerous or overly time consuming. And it does not have to be in any set format other than something that you will refer to and adjust as things change.

The two simple steps that follow will get you started on a career or business plan.

Conduct a Gap Analysis

This is simply the process of working out where you are now and where you want to be *(your goals)*. Easy!

Once you have done that, identify the difference between the two – that's the gap you need your plan to address. Every gap provides an opportunity for you to bridge it, to make up the difference between where you are now in your knowledge, skills, and experience, and where you want or need to be.

Write an Action Plan

Every gap you identify can be addressed with an action. It might be a task, someone you need to meet, or something you need to know, learn, practice or do.

This list of what you to need to do and when you need to do them is your plan. *(Bonus points if you prioritize what's most important!)*

How you document your plan can be as complex or as simple as you want. It should be in a way that you find easy to manage; a spreadsheet, a Word document, an app, a task list, or a good old-fashioned notebook, whatever works for you. You're working from home, so it could involve a whiteboard, or a drawing stuck on the wall or the fridge. Whatever you will find easy to refer to, tick off and actually do.

And that's as complicated as it needs to be. Have a plan so you know what you need to do and when you need to do it.

Your goals are the 'why' you need to do it. Your plan is the 'how' you will achieve the goals you have set yourself.

76. Get a mentor

Originating from Greek mythology you'll hear the term mentor used today in various situations, including business, sport and education. Whatever the circumstances, a mentor describes someone knowledgeable, skilled or experienced who can provide guidance to someone who wants to develop in the mentor's field of expertise.

A mentor isn't necessarily an older or more senior person in an organization's hierarchy. For instance, when you change company or career it's very likely that people younger than you will have more expertise. Or if you are looking to master some new piece of technology, your best bet may be a teenage mentor who can quickly figure it out. *(I confess I had to defer to my teenage nieces to help me with my Instagram account!)*

Mentors are a secret weapon in career and personal development. They are absolutely essential to your career when you work from home. They are important to help you stay in touch with what is happening outside of your own four walls and benchmark your skills and expertise. A mentor can provide you with a broader perspective on many aspects of your work, career, and options. A mentoring relationship can provide you with feedback, fresh ideas, approaches, knowledge, expertise, and advice.

A mentor can provide you with:

- knowledge

- guidance on your career, an organization's internal politics, the market and your skills or communication style *(to name just a few opportunities)*

- a sounding board – to discuss how you handled a situation or how you should tackle something in the future

- access to networks, and

- honest, valuable feedback.

The benefits are numerous and invaluable in helping you reach your potential, whatever your field or current level of achievement. Oprah mentored 'Dr. Phil'. Michael Jordan, Roger Federer, and David Beckham have all acknowledged their mentors as being important to their success. Any top achiever you can think of will have had a mentor or coach – someone to guide, counsel and provide advice. Someone who can look at their performance, provide a different perspective, and advise strategies.

It's the same in business. Leaders from all types of backgrounds credit one or several mentors for their guidance along the way. Entrepreneur Sir Richard Branson of Virgin brand fame acknowledges Sir Frederick Laker, a British airline entrepreneur, as his mentor, and the late Dave Thomas, the founder of Wendy's hamburger chain, was mentored for many years by KFC's Harland "Colonel" Sanders.

The fact that these famous, talented and successful people made use of the skills and expertise of others illustrates that having a mentor is a legitimate, not to mention successful, strategy to develop your career.

Identifying an area for development and finding a mentor is part of developing your career plan. By the time you approach a potential mentor you should have identified what you want to learn from them and have decided that the person you are going to approach will be able to help you.

There are a number of different types of people and ways you can approach a *prospective mentor.*

Mentor Target 1: Someone you know

If you approach someone you have an established relationship with you can get straight to a discussion about the area that you are seeking help with. You don't even have to use the "m" word *(mentor!).*

Here are a couple of approaches you could try:

"I'm currently working on improving my (insert your skill of choice), and I was wondering if we could catch-up so I could ask you a few questions about how you...? Given that I work from home but still want to work on developing my skills I'd really appreciate if we could have a call about..."

And another:

"It's been really helpful when we've talked previously about xyz; I have a few career options that I'm weighing up and I wonder if you'd have time for a call?"

Who could resist? These approaches cover why you want some of their valuable time and how they can help. If you ask in this way and do get turned down, usually it will be for a genuine reason, such as time or work pressures. Not because they don't want to help you. At the very least you will have represented yourself as a professional who is serious about your career.

If they agree, it could be a one-off conversation regarding the issue you approach them about, or the beginning of a longer term mentoring relationship.

You don't have to formally ask if the person will mentor you. A follow-up thank-you call, a second meeting… you start to build a relationship by catching up regularly, and before you know it: you've got them. *(As a mentor that is!)*

Mentor Target 2: Your manager is moving on

If your manager is moving on to a new opportunity, you have a good rapport, and there are things you would still like to learn from them, formalize a mentoring relationship so you can stay in touch. I once had a manager resign six weeks after I took a job specifically so I could work with them (sigh…), but we remained in contact for many years, and I still had the opportunity to learn from her. Try asking:

"I am so pleased you have this opportunity. But I'll miss the chance to work with you and learn more about your approach to XYZ. Do you think you might be able to continue working with me on this as a mentor?"

Formalizing your relationship before they walk out the door makes it legitimate for you to keep in contact even if they're up to their necks in their new role. They will remember the commitment they made to you.

Mentor Target 3: Someone you don't know (well)

It's probably best to have some vague association with the person and not just randomly approach senior managers trying to land a mentor. This association – whether you work in the same organization or business unit, someone has recommended you to approach them, or you have a work issue in common – whatever it is, is your introduction as to why you are getting in touch and will allow you to establish your credibility.

Once you have done this, proceed as you would with someone you know better, explaining why you want to speak to them, what you are trying to learn, and how you think they can help. People will be flattered when you ask for their help. The type of person that you are likely to want to learn from is usually the type of person who wants to help.

The worst thing that can happen is that they say no and you are no worse off. Just ask. As long as you do so professionally, there is no reason not to give it a go!

A mentor will take you, and your request to work with them, seriously if you can describe where you are in your career, work or business and what you want to learn and why. You need to assure them that you are serious and seeking their help for the right reasons. They will also want to know that you are genuinely interested in and committed to the process.

Mentors are a key asset in advancing your skills, knowledge, and career development. Unlike other opportunities that are not as readily accessible when you work from home, a mentor is only a phone call away. Get one.

77. Identify sponsors and influencers

There are people who influence the success of your career or business that you may not even know about; influential people who speak about you or your business to others. They can sing your praises or recommend you for a position, project or other opportunities. Sometimes you may never even know who these people are who have spoken well of you.

When people have a talented contact or know a person that is a suitable fit for an opportunity they will often make recommendations. It's a way for them to give back to their network and contacts. And it's good for you, too.

When you work from home and out of sight, being top of mind with people who can impact your opportunities is imperative so that you can be the person they recommend.

If you can identify the people who are potential sponsors or influencers, keep them informed about the progress of your work and career. They could be previous managers, clients, or people from other parts of your organization who you work with on projects. Building your reputation to realize sponsors (and opportunities) is one of a number of excellent reasons why it is important to develop and maintain your network.

You have a phone and all sorts of technology to connect with people, so there is no reason why you can't do this just as well when you work from home. For instance, stay in contact with previous managers or colleagues, and keep them up-to-date with your current work achievements. A quick call, a couple of lines in an email, or an occasional coffee when you go to the office is all it takes to keep the lines of communication open.

If the people who can influence outcomes for you know about your current skills and achievements, they are much more likely to speak well of you to others. You never know, they may even have an opportunity for you in the future.

Identify potential sponsors and influencers, build relationships, demonstrate your capability, and keep in touch with them as part of your career development.

78. Invest in learning

There are two key crucial investments in learning: time and money. Investing in both for ongoing learning is crucial for developing your career.

A study by Professor John Field on the topic 'Is lifelong learning making a difference?' found that *"Adult learning influences people's income and employability, as well as the attitudes and behaviors that affect people's mental well-being."*[i] That sounds good enough for me!

Your company may or may not have formal training and coaching programs. Excellent if you have access to them. But don't totally rely on this for your ongoing development. The opportunities to learn provided by your organization may relate to your current role, but will they provide you with the knowledge and skills you need for your career goals? For your next job? If they do, then fabulous. Use every learning opportunity that is relevant for you (and your career plan). If they don't, then look further afield for the options available to you.

If you don't have access to learning through your current role, then responsibility for learning is definitely up to you.

It can teach you new ways of working, expand your thinking, stimulate your creativity and open you up to new possibilities. The time and money invested to achieve this can be recouped many times over if it leads to a new role or client.

And it's not just about signing up for training courses *(although this is one of your options).*

Here are some other ways to learn new stuff and keep across new thinking and developments:

- Read – articles, journals, books, blogs.

- Enrol in online courses – there are many free ones offered by universities, such as Harvard, and other credible organizations.

- Subscribe to associations and interest groups to stay up-to-date with developments in your industry or area of expertise.

- Attend conferences and networking events.

- Get a mentor.

- Engage a coach.

- Listen to podcasts.

- Attend webinars.

- Network.

There are endless ways you can spend your time and money. *(Travel and shoes are just a couple that spring to mind, is that just me?)* The options for how you spend your days and cash are never-ending, including the basics like feeding yourself and your family. They are all competing with the discretionary investment in learning.

But think about it this way: you are a great investment! And the person who should be most interested in investing in you? Who is likely to get the biggest benefits? Who can enjoy the process of learning? As well as reap the rewards in your future career? You!

Investment in learning is an investment in you and your career.

79. Network

Deep relationships, built on trust and respect, are necessary to access information and ideas, and to learn new skills. These can be developed with the people you work with and through your network.

Putting time and energy into building and maintaining a network can have a variety of benefits for your career. A strong network can help you:

- learn new information or skills
- discover ideas and enjoy stimulating discussions
- find out how to do things better or differently
- know who to go to in an organization, and
- identify future job opportunities and promotions.

The recruitment industry tells us that a significant number of job vacancies are never advertised, and that people access the hidden employment market through their networks. If you don't have a network to provide you with information, referrals, or to let other people know who you are, it severely limits your career options. When you work from home these potential benefits are important in order to continually perform at your best and open up opportunities for the future.

You can get to know people really well over the phone and by maintaining regular contact with them. In one role I was working extremely closely with a colleague based in Perth on the other side of Australia *(that's a long way and 3 hours' time difference in the summer)*. Often we would speak multiple times a day. We were so used to our communication being by phone that it was actually a little weird when we would occasionally see each other at a meeting. We no longer work together, but Brett is definitely part of my long-term network.

Some people measure their networking success by the number of functions they attend and the number of business cards they collect. But when push comes to shove and you need advice or help in the future, can you rely on people you met once to help you out? Will they take time from their busy schedule and give you the best of their advice? Maybe. Maybe not. *(I'm betting on the not.)*

To be fair if the only connection you have is a quick handshake, a business-card swap and maybe a LinkedIn invitation, there really isn't a strong relationship to fall back on. Alternatively, if you build mutually beneficial relationships with the people you meet and work with, they are much more likely to support you when you need it. I can definitely give Brett a call if I need to chat about something and vice versa.

When it comes to your network, include people you have worked with previously – colleagues, managers, suppliers or customers – and make the effort to meet new people to expand your contacts. *(Note: this may require you to leave home occasionally!)*

To build and maintain your network, you can:

- Identify people whom you trust, respect, and are good at what they do, and that you would like to have more contact with.

- Introduce yourself to people you want to meet, and prepare questions to help facilitate interesting or constructive conversations.

- Create worthwhile reasons to maintain contact. Introduce them to other contacts or send them information about areas of common interest.

Importantly, enjoy the conversations and contacts with the people in your network. The social interaction can be all-important when you are at home a lot of the time.

Network and you'll be working on your career at the same time.

80. Follow up after a networking event

Well done, you! You've been to a networking event. Met some great people. Swapped some business cards. Introduced yourself to someone you wanted to meet. Caught up with some people you know. Heard some new ideas. Got a little bit inspired. What now?

Been there. Done that. Networking ticked off the career to-do list? Afraid not. Because unless you actually follow up and look after the connections you make, it really is just a tick-the-box activity.

If you've made the effort to leave the house and meet people, follow up to build on the connections that you've made. Also apply the inspiration or ideas that you got from the event, and don't let the time that you invested go to waste.

After you have been to a networking event here's a few things you can do.

Connect with people you met

If there were people you found areas of common interest with and swapped contact details with, then connect with them. Preferably within 48 hours. Send them a request to connect on LinkedIn. This ensures you have the correct contact details for them in the future. Personalize the invitation reminding them of where you met and something you discussed. Alternatively send them an email to follow through on the connection.

Follow up on commitments

Did you make any commitments like *"I'll send you a link to..."* or *"We must catch-up for coffee"*? If you did, make sure you follow through. Jump on the email and send the link or propose a time for that coffee catch-up. It's great for your personal credibility and will significantly increase the chances that the person you met moves from a connection to a contact.

Write down your ideas

Maybe it's just me, but when I hear speakers I get a ton of ideas. People I should contact, information that they talk about that I want to look up and read about myself... All sorts of things. Write yourself some notes and reminders as soon as you can so that you don't lose those precious ideas.

Take action

It's inspiring to get ideas; it's powerful to act on them. If someone makes a suggestion, you hear something that you think you can try, or you get a brilliant idea – act on it.

Plan your next networking event

Keep those connections, contacts, tips, and ideas coming.

Career development is a continual process and there are always new things to learn.

Networking is a great way to work on your career.

81. Be professionally active online

Through the magic of the Internet, you are only a few keystrokes away from being active in professional forums anywhere in the world. Who you are and what you do will dictate which ones are right for you.

If you can go to professional events it's tremendous, they are an important part of networking, connecting, and learning. But the type and frequency of events may be limited by how much time you have to attend, how far away they are, and even how much they cost. They can also be one-off events or too infrequent to really get to know people.

You can augment your face-to-face networking with involvement in your choice of the myriad online forums available. Whether it's through groups on LinkedIn or through professional or industry associations, your involvement can be part of your career development.

They provide a forum where you have the opportunity to keep up with current thinking and see the types of questions and topics that people are talking about. They provide the opportunity for you to share, test your ideas, and establish connections with others, without being restricted by time or location. You never know whom you might be engaging with or what you might learn.

Being respectful, thoughtful, and generous with your contributions can do much to build your credibility and enhance your professional reputation.

82. Recognize when it is time to move on

You might be in exactly the right role now, particularly given the opportunity you have to work from home. But things change.

When you work remotely, you can't physically see who is coming and going to the office, if there are any unusual behaviors, such as, closed-door meetings or strained expressions. But if you stay connected with people you can keep your antenna up and recognize if there is anything going on that may precipitate your need to make a career or job change. Lost customer contracts, declining industries, corporate takeovers, and many other things can lead to changes in the workplace.

On the other hand you may initiate a change in your role, career or business. Opportunities might present themselves or you might engineer them based on your career plan. Being able to recognize when it's time to move on provides you with control and choice about what you do next.

To manage your career moves, consider:

- Putting up your hand and being prepared to take up new opportunities when they present themselves.

- Actively keeping across what is going on and recognize times of change.

- Evaluating if the time is right to move and understand how you make successful decisions.

- Moving on if things go bad and can't be fixed. For instance, if you are working for a bad manager, it can be just as soul-destroying to work for them from home as it was in the office. Sometimes worse, because you have more time to stew on the situation. Do what is right for you.

- Developing options and alternatives before you need them. Have a Plan B.

The truth is there are plenty of roles where you can negotiate working from home as part of your conditions. Don't get sucked into staying in a bad situation or not taking advantage of an opportunity because you don't think you have a choice.

Stay alert and recognize when it's time to move on for the future you choose or the present that you want to experience now.

VIII. WELL-BEING *(how to look after you)*

It doesn't matter how much you get paid, promoted or receive accolades for your work, if you don't look after yourself, you won't be able to enjoy it.

When you work from home, regardless of whether you are an employee or not, the person in charge of looking after you is… you. Your well-being is absolutely essential to achieve and maintain career and personal success – not a luxury. Whatever your personal circumstances, no matter how busy you are, you need to prioritize the things that help you look after you.

On an airplane, the safety briefing always includes instructions to fit your own oxygen mask first so that you are able to help others. In hospital-emergency rooms, clinical staff often refer to the quote from *The House of God*, 'take your own pulse first' so that they are able to look after patients. Or in the words of comedic genius Lucille Ball, *"Love yourself first and everything else falls into line. You really have to love yourself to get anything done in this world."* Airlines, hospitals, Lucille Ball, everyone agrees… you need to look after yourself first!

It also has a positive impact on your work and career. When you look after yourself, others notice how you manage and present yourself. Your reputation is enhanced if you are cool, calm and collected, rather than flustered, out of control and frantic. Time spent on activities can be an investment in building your network. Playing sport, being creative, even learning about wine and food can help you find things in common with others and help you engage in the small talk that is such an important part of building relationships. Activities you enjoy are not an indulgence; they are part of what life is about.

A successful athlete spends time cross-training to build physical fitness and to complement the core skills that are required in their discipline. When you work from home, cross-training involves eating well, exercise, moving regularly, managing your hours, interacting with others, and taking time out for yourself.

These are just a few of the tips in this section to help you prioritize your well-being and look after you.

83. Move it (that means you!)

It is pretty well universally agreed that moving your body is essential. For physical health, mental well-being, bone density, disease prevention, lowering glucose levels, and pain management... You name it. It seems moving can help it! The list of reasons to make us get off our butts and move seems endless – and it's pointless to argue about it. Even if you're having a busy day, the fact is that we all need to make time to move.

Those of us who work from home have no commute, no meetings across town or elsewhere in the building, and the freedom to work interrupted and become immersed in a project it can be a challenge to make ourselves move as much as we should *(or at all!)*. Until I started actively making myself move, I found I was sometimes only taking 173 steps a day!

The trick is to have a routine to make it happen. As philosopher Will Durant said when summarizing the writings of Aristotle, *"We are what we repeatedly do. Excellence, then, is a not an act, but a habit."* The Adamedes' version of this is *"Make moving a habit and you will be excellent."* Or at least feel quite virtuous and everything else will be a bonus!

A 2017 study tracked 8000 people and after four years it found that people who had the most and longest uninterrupted periods of time sitting had an increased likelihood of dying[i].

What? It's not just about feeling virtuous anymore... this is life and death stuff!

The good news is that they also found that getting up every 30 minutes can help. They think. A slightly earlier study by the University of Utah, School of Medicine suggested two minutes of walking every hour as being beneficial.[ii] Whichever study you look at, and however long they suggest, all the research suggests that moving is a requirement to living.

And then there is the need to look after our eyes and give them a break from looking at screens. The old 20-20-20 rule is often recommended to avoid eyestrain. Take a 20-second break every 20 minutes, and look at something that is 20 feet away. *(That's about six metres in metric, but the 20-20-6 rule doesn't sound quite as cool.)*

It turns out that all those wellness recommendations that are in your company's health and well-being training are actually good ideas. And even if you work for yourself now, you are sure to have come across all these good ideas in the past. *(I'll be back in a minute I need to walk to the kitchen, grab a glass of water, and look out the window…)*

Right, I'm back. Quick, right? No one will notice if you take the breaks you need to look after yourself. I promise you that all of your emails will still be sitting in your inbox when you get back *(and there might even be a few more for good measure!)*. If you are worried about missing an urgent call, take your phone with you *(they're pretty sophisticated these days and you can carry them around!)*.

While many of the tips recommended to office workers don't apply when you work from home (such as taking the stairs in the office or getting off the bus one stop early), there are plenty of little habits you can get into that will make a difference. Consider these:

- Walk when you talk on the phone.

- Get up and go to the bathroom or refill your water in the kitchen every half hour *(if you drink enough water, you'll need to get up to go to the bathroom!)*

- Set an alarm to remind yourself to move.

- Integrate some household chores into your day *(there is nothing like the annoying beep of the washing machine or microwave to motivate some movement. They can be really, really annoying!)*.

- Open the front door and step outside for a few deep breaths and some fresh air.

- Pick up your laptop and move to another part of the house.

- Put five-minute breaks between meetings in your calendar *(and use them to move, not squeeze in another email.)*.

- Leave the house and work somewhere else for a while *(you get to move and have the potential for coffee and some actual face-to-face human interaction)*.

- Track your steps and set yourself a daily target.

I confess I am a long way from perfect on this, but I started walking when I am on the phone, and now when the phone rings I automatically stand up. Sometimes I need to run back through the house to access information or share screens, but it certainly helps my daily step tally.

The bottom line is that there seems to be a strong correlation between moving and staying alive. Good enough.

These are all little things but if you add them up and do them every day they are habits to help you move.

84. Leave the house once a day

As tempting as it is to enjoy the peace and quiet of working from home and pump out work hour after hour, day after day, it can be a bit isolating. As nice as your dedicated office space might be, even if you love your work it's good to have some other sensory input.

Leaving the house once a day will provide a break from your work, get you up and moving, provide you with some different stimuli and potentially even other people to talk to. All of which will get you physically moving and positively contributing to your feeling of well-being. You might be able to grab a coffee that is better than the one you can make yourself *(even if it's to-go you need to leave the house to get it!)*. And you are much more likely to get some inspiration when you take a break from your work environment.

There is no reason to feel guilty about leaving your desk. Your office colleagues are picking up coffees and lunches, running errands and having impromptu meetings or chats about which series they are binge watching at the moment. They are not tied to their desks. And you do not need to be either.

Build the time it takes to leave the house, even for a short time, into your daily schedule. Here are some ideas for reasons to leave the house:

- Exercise before work starts or any time of the day that you have factored into your schedule.
- Grab a coffee (or drink of your choice).
- Walk around the block while you are making calls.
- Have lunch in a café.
- Buy some groceries.
- Attend a networking event.
- Visit a client.
- Pick up dry cleaning, children or do another household errand.

I'm sure you can think of many more! None of these are incredibly time consuming *(or don't have to be)* and can fit into your workday. Worst-case scenario: walk to the mailbox and have a peek inside. It's highly unlikely there will be anything in there, but at least you will have moved and left the house!

85. Schedule exercise

When I asked my personal trainer, Jordan Peters (JP), about the importance of exercise, he said, *"Fitness, if done properly, allows you to use your body and mind to its fullest potential."* Surely this is what we all want?

I have absolutely no medical expertise at all but I read all the same stuff that you do about the numerous benefits of exercise. It has physical-health benefits, mental-health benefits, builds strength, helps prevent diseases, boosts everything from energy to memory, and improves sleep as well as skin tone. And that's not all. So for the purposes of this tip, let's work on the assumption that you need to exercise.

The challenge when you work from home is to make sure you do. With the flexibility that being at home brings there should be plenty of time to work a run, walk or gym session into your day. Theoretically that is. The reality though is that you sit down, start work, have meetings and phone calls, and before you know it the day is gone. You may have had an extremely productive day, but your exercise plans went by the wayside.

The only way to make sure you have the time to exercise is to… make time to exercise! Everyone I talked to, from the East Coast of the US, to London and Sydney, all had basically the same advice: schedule exercise into your day. It just makes sense. Scheduling your time is a great way to get stuff done and be productive when you're at home. And your exercise, which is important to you, is one of the things that you need to include in your schedule.

Sure, there are days when it's hard *(I could probably write another book called 101 Excuses for Not Going to the Gym!)*, but when I think I'm too busy or any number of other legitimately good excuses, I remember the immortal words of JP, my personal trainer: *"Shut up and do it anyway!"*

86. Remember to eat

While you are taking your breaks, exercising, giving your eyes a break from your screen, and actually working, remember to factor some time into your day to eat. Walk to the kitchen, grab your snack, sit outside, and take a good look into the distance while you eat it. Then you're good to go back to work and be productive. Extra credit if you add a walk around the garden or the block! Seriously though, we know how quickly a day can go by when you are working from home, and nutrition is just one of the things that you need to take care of to look after yourself.

Some people have told me they are challenged by the proximity and temptation of the fridge on the days when they work from home. Others say that they get into the zone, have meeting after meeting with no scheduled breaks or one interruption after another and it's suddenly 3pm and they are sitting with their legs crossed *(you can use your imagination about why – and you need to take breaks for that too!)* and haven't eaten anything since the piece of toast they had hours earlier.

I had a lesson about looking after myself when I was managing a situation that required meetings, briefings, phone calls, follow-ups – one after the other. This went on for two days and I just went into 'crisis' mode. I bounced from call to call, and I did not prioritize myself. On the second day at 3pm I had a 10-minute break, rushed to the fridge, grabbed a yogurt *(not checking the Best Before date)* and practically snorted it down. I immediately felt so sick I had to go to the bathroom and throw up, grabbed a glass of water and was actually congratulating myself that I managed to make my next teleconference call on time. This happened on a Friday. The following Wednesday I was made redundant.

"More fool I" was my reflection after the event. Of course, you need to do everything you can, and go above and beyond when you need to, but it shouldn't be to the detriment of your health.

Skipping meals or eating fast food is not a plan. Not a good one anyway. And the experts tell us that good nutrition is important for concentration and productivity, let alone any of that general good-health, staying-alive stuff that is kind of in our best interest.

To make it easier to eat healthily on a workday, consider these food ideas:

- Grab-and-go snack packs with nuts or cut-up vegetables
- Yogurt *(check the best before date!)*
- Boiled eggs
- Leftovers from dinner the night before (you can also freeze them in one-meal portion sizes)
- A full fruit bowl
- A well-stocked fridge and cupboard, filled with ingredients you can throw into a bowl together. Hey presto! You have a healthy meal.

There are a lot of quick and healthy eating options, it just takes a bit of planning to be organized and put yourself first.

Be prepared and then… just remember to eat!

87. Lunch away from your desk

There may be no one at the next desk to be envious of *(or complain)* about the aroma of your lunch or any health risks associated with the germs that might be on a shared keyboard in a flexible working environment... but that doesn't mean you should eat lunch at your desk when you work from home *(that applies to breakfast and dinner as well!)*.

I'm the first to admit that I have eaten lunch at my desk more times than I should have. The reasons are always the same: no break between meetings; a never-ending inbox of emails; a constantly ringing phone; and, probably the worst reason of all, so I can spend my 'break' on social media. *(I'm not the only one, right?)* I've had plenty of crumbs in the keyboard and if I'm honest I've probably had to spend more time cleaning it than I've saved through the multi-tasking or working and munching at the same time.

Meal times are a chance to have a mental break, move, grab some rays of sunshine, and focus on what you are going to eat. It's also the ideal opportunity to leave the house and interact with some human beings face to face.

The great thing about working from home is you can schedule your breaks at a time to suit you. Unless you have meetings you just can't avoid, you can decide to have your lunch break in the middle of the morning or late in the afternoon; whatever works for you. Plan when you are going to take your lunch break, and make sure you include that time in your schedule. Every day.

Even a short break – say, a visit to the kitchen to grab some food, then eating it at the dining-room table – ticks a lot of boxes. It gives your eyes a rest, gets you moving, and provides you with a break to refresh or contemplate your priorities. *(Double points if you go outside and get some fresh air and steps at the same time!)*

Your food choices are up to you, too. Make something yummy for dinner and have the leftovers for lunch the next day. Pop out to your favorite coffee shop. Prepare something fresh and delicious as part of your break. Arrange to meet a friend or a colleague. All of a sudden, breaking for lunch goes from being an irritating interruption to something you can really look forward to.

It takes discipline to tear yourself away from whatever urgent thing you have to work on and lunch away from your desk – but it is a good use of your time.

88. Manage your hours

Hidden here as tip number 88 between lunching away from your desk and connecting with human beings, is possibly the most important and challenging tip of all: manage your hours.

It seems like many people who work from home feel that they need to be available 24/7, as a trade-off for the flexibility, peace and quiet, no commute, and many other benefits of working from home. It can be difficult to manage the boundaries between work hours and personal time when you work from home.

One person who works from home on the east coast of the US, said, *"I find it more difficult to draw boundaries... I could work 14-hour days without breaks."* Another, who runs her own business from London, said, *"It's very, very hard to switch off. There's always something you could be doing."* And another based in Australia admitted, *"I do tend to work more hours – log on early and work late."*

And research backs this up. The 2017 *'Working anytime, anywhere: The effects on the world of work'* report found that the disadvantages of what they term Telework/ICT mobile work (T/ICTM) are *"the tendency to lead to longer working hours, to create an overlap between paid work and personal life (work–home interference), and to result in work intensification."* [iii]

In May 2019, the World Economic Forum reported that working from home is characterized by early starts and late finishes.[iv] This is backed up by research conducted by Heejung Chung from the University of Kent in the UK, and colleagues in Germany and the UK. They found that *"when workers have more autonomy over their working hours they are likely to increase the hours they work."*[v]

If you are looking for just one reason why working longer hours is not a good idea, try this one. A French study, published in June 2019, found that long working hours (LWH) are a potential risk factor for stroke. They defined this as working 10 hours or more a day for 50 days or more a year. It found a *"significant association between stroke and exposure to LWH for 10 years or more."* [vi]

I rest my case: you need to manage your hours.

We've talked about some of these ideas in other tips, but I think they are well worth highlighting and building into the way you manage your hours:

- Set your working hours – even if they are going to vary, have a plan ahead of time, and know when you are going to start and finish work each day.

- Structure your day and have a plan so you know you can do what you need to do.

- Have a dedicated work area, ideally with a door, to help separate work and home.

- If you can, turn off your phone at the end of your working day. Or at least put it on silent.

- Don't be a slave to the inbox. When you're done for the day, you're done.

- Work during the most productive part of your day.

- If you need to work late make sure you have taken a break during the day. Or work a short day the next day. Or the one before. *(It all depends on how good you are with your planning!)*

- Make commitments with others so that you have to finish work for the day. It will help with that whole work versus home balance thing as well.

- Exercise at the beginning, middle, or the end of the day.

- Take your breaks.

- Leave the house once a day.

- Use an out-of-office email response if you need to let people know you are not available.

- Turn off your computer and leave it in your office at the end of the working day.

- Better yet, close the door to your office to signal to you and everyone else in your household that you have finished work.

If you've done what you planned to do and there are no 'emergencies' that you need to deal with – just stop work for the day. It will still be there tomorrow.

Just because you *could* do more, does not mean you *should* do more. There is always more to do. Learning how to manage your hours is one of these things. And on that note I am going to finish this tip, turn off my lap-top, close my office door, and have some 'me' time. I'll be back to write Tip 89 in the morning. It can wait.

89. Interact with human beings (in person)

One of the negatives of working from home can be that you feel lonely or isolated. The lack of distractions can make you super productive, but it can get lonely.

When you work from home one to two days a week, then spend a few days a week visiting clients or going to the office, the sound of silence at home can be golden. The peace and quiet can be a welcome opportunity to get work done. But day-in day-out, every day, and the thought of some office chitchat as a distraction and connecting with some actual people can be very welcome.

A study conducted by Buffer reported that 21% of respondents, both employees and freelancers, said that loneliness was their number-one struggle with working remotely.[vii] Another study by Randstad US and Apartment Guide surveyed that 43% of Gen-Z workers admitted that they get lonely when working from home.[viii]

Phone calls, emails, messages, video chats and conference calls are great ways to keep in touch, but they do not provide quite the same level of connectedness with others. They do not replace face-to-face catch-ups where there are greater nuances in body language, which add to communication.

Not all work-from-homers feel isolated or lonely. On a LinkedIn post about remote work, author and coach Donald J "DJ" Sebastian commented, *"In 25+ years of working remotely, I never once felt lonely or isolated. My days were filled with conversations with customers, teammates and business partners. The local coffee shops served as a respite when I wanted to be near other people. An impending business trip afforded me opportunities to be surrounded by hundreds of travelers."*

To avoid the isolation, like DJ did, there are a number of ways to connect with human beings in person during your workday. Here are some ideas:

Make some meetings with colleagues or clients face-to-face –even if you could do them by phone. It might take a little bit more time, but it will help you develop rapport, build some variety into your schedule, and provide you with some human interaction.

Leave the house once a day – even if it is just for a personal errand or a coffee. If you leave the house you have a much greater chance for a conversation than if you don't. Asking your barista how their day is going, having a few words with a sales associate, or wishing someone a good day can all help you feel connected with other humans.

Work from an office one day a week – either for the company you work for or in a co-working space. According to a 2017 Gallup study conducted in the US, workers who spend 60–80% of their time away from the office were the most engaged.[ix] This means, working just one day a week from the office can make you happier!

Relocate somewhere else – take your laptop and work in a coffee shop, a park, the beach *(although sand can be a problem)* or anywhere where there are other people around. You don't have to be restricted by Wi-Fi access – just use the hotspot on your phone and you can work anywhere.

Get involved in a local activity – whether it's volunteering, networking or catching up with neighbors or friends, create your own 'team' – people that you catch-up with regularly.

Connecting with people isn't restricted to being work related. Look at your whole schedule and where it is going to work for you. Use the flexibility perk of working from home so that you can make it work for you.

Avoid feeling lonely or isolated, and interact with actual human beings in person!

90. Plan meals in advance

It can come as a surprise to those who don't work from home that meal planning is an issue for those of us who do. *"The kitchen,"* they correctly point out, *"is literally a few seconds from your office. What is the big deal?"*

The reality though is that it's easy to just keep working away, having short breaks, and not leaving yourself enough time to make something yummy and healthy – let alone get to the store to buy the supplies you need. If you don't have a convenience store with a range of ready-made meals just around the corner or easy-to-arrange home delivery, the only option is to do it yourself.

Planning your meals in advance is one way to help you look after yourself while you work. If you are one of those super-organized people who prep your meals for the week in advance this tip will seem obvious! But for those of us who are less disciplined *(that's me)*, a little bit of a plan makes a difference between eating or not; being healthy or not; or making a last-minute dash to the store or not.

To help you plan, consider:

- Getting food boxes with all the ingredients and recipes delivered straight to your door.

- Stocking up the cupboard with options that can quickly be turned into a meal.

- Writing a meal plan once a week, then buying everything you need in advance. *(This is my plan every week, but I think three days in advance is my PB!)*

- Freezing leftovers in individual servings, so they can be quickly reheated in the microwave for lunch.

- Cooking double the amount, so that you can have leftovers for the next night or freeze *(see above)* for those busy days when you can't or don't want to cook.

- Building a trip to the store into your schedule – it's a good reason to leave the house, gives you a break from work, and the opportunity to buy fresh food.

- Using a slow cooker – prep at lunch time and have it ready to devour at the end of the day when you'd rather do anything except cook.

- Thinking about lunch tomorrow when you are planning dinner. Something extra thrown on the grill *(or BBQ, as we call it here in Australia)* is very convenient to add to a salad or turn into a yummy sandwich the next day.

- Asking for help. Just because you are the person who is at home all the time, meal preparation should not always fall to you.

Planning meals in advance *(even if the plan is to eat out)* can help you eat healthily, remove some stress from your day, and work in with your schedule. It helps you look after you.

91. Change your environment

Scroll through hashtags like #workfromhome, #remotework, #workfromanywhere and the like on your choice of social-media platform. Your feed will be filled with photos of people proudly sharing the non-office locations they work from.

Cafes, parks and gardens, with views of beaches, rivers, lakes and trees all feature very heavily. *(There are also plenty of pictures of dogs and cats getting in the way or loving having their humans at home.)* The sub-text of these location shots is pretty much, *"How lucky am I?"* or *"How good is this?"* and *"This makes work so much better."*

With no one looking over your shoulder and technology that you can pick up and take with you, the flexibility to work in different places throughout the day is yours. No matter how much you love your dedicated work space at home, staring at the same four walls can become a little less than stimulating – to say the least.

Sure there are things you can't do in a public place, such as taking confidential calls and working on commercially sensitive documents or something really detailed where two screens are a must. But there is plenty you can do while you're out and about: reading, thinking, planning, emails, and writing to-do lists, presentations and papers. If you don't want to work on a Wi-Fi hot spot or there isn't one where you want to work, take one with you by using your phone or a mobile Wi-Fi device.

My goddaughter Grace wrote all of her English papers for her final year of high school in her local café. She would order a cup of tea, set the alarm on her phone for an hour and write as much as she could in that time – a great way to be efficient and enjoy a change of scenery. There's no reason we can't do that when we work from home.

I know that I am guilty of sitting down at my desk, beavering away at what needs to be done, and not even thinking about working elsewhere. When you are busy, the time it takes to move elsewhere can seem like an unnecessary interruption. But if you schedule some work you can do outside the office, you'll get a break while you relocate to your new space and the stimulation of being in a new environment. *(When I do this, it usually involves a coffee!)*

Even if you don't leave the house *(extra bonus points if you do)* and just move to a balcony or the garden, there are still benefits to be enjoyed. Some fresh air, a gentle breeze, and some rays of sunshine may all help your productivity or creativity.

One of the greatest freedoms of working from home is the flexibility. Use yours to be where you want to work, and be able to say, *"How good is this?"*

92. Sick? Take the day off

If you work for yourself no work usually means no pay which is quite an incentive to keep working through coughs and sniffles. If you are an employee and work from home you may feel that you can't justify taking the day off. It's not like there are any co-workers that you could infect.

But you do need to look after yourself and common sense should prevail. If you need rest to recover – take some time off. If you are feeling so bad that you are going to make mistakes – take some time off. If you are on medication, which you should not be taking when you are working – take some time off.

Just don't fall into the trap of thinking that because you are already at home that you can keep on powering on simply because you don't have to travel into work.

If you are an employee, use your sick leave. If you do work for yourself, and this is tricky, you need to factor the fact that you can't work every single day into your fees and charges. You need to be able to take sick days *(and vacations, too!)*.

If you are sick, take the day off, tell anyone at work who needs to know, put an out-of-office reply on your email, turn your phone off *(or at the very least put it on silent)*, and take the day off.

Remember you are the most valuable asset for your career and need to be looked after.

93. Pay yourself back time

Tight deadlines, massive projects, and the demands of your customers or boss can all add up to early-morning starts, late-night finishes, skipped lunches and weekend work. This can be a short-term peak or reasonably lengthy period or season when the pace of work is hectic and the hours long.

Peaks and troughs happen, and sometimes the reality is that you need to put in some long hours. The trick is to make sure long hours don't become your new normal. It can lead to stress for you, impact on your relationships with others, and cause you to resent your work.

A short term surge in work pressure and hours can be a buzz; it gets the adrenaline going and can be interesting, satisfying and exciting. Do it for too long, however, and you are at risk of burnout. Or at the very least it becomes the new normal, and expected by you and your colleagues, clients or boss.

The big effort that you put in may not only impact you but other people who are important to you. Allocating time for the people who support us is important to acknowledge their contributions and say thank you.

A career is more like a marathon than a sprint, and you need to pace yourself. Unless you consciously decide that you want to work longer than you did before a busy period, you need to create a trough and dial the pressure down. And you need to do this without feeling guilty about it.

It's most unlikely that your boss or clients will come to you and say, *"I see you've been working some longer hours, why don't you finish at lunchtime on Friday?"* It's up to you to take advantage of some of this work-from-home flexibility and pay yourself back the time that you are owed; or at least some of it.

Ease off and make time for yourself, family and friends. Start later, finish early, add some time to your coffee break, go to the gym or for a walk in the middle of the day, arrange a long lunch with a friend. *(I'm sure you can think of more ideas if you put a little thought into it.)*

Paying yourself back time is only fair to yourself and the people you care about. If you want justification from a work perspective it gives you time to re-energize, to be ready for the next busy period, and to do your best work. But the best reason is to do it just for you.

94. Claim expenses

Unless you are independently wealthy or have significant inheritance expectations, there is a pretty reasonable chance that money is one of the main reasons you work. One area where the line can blur between work and home is in claiming expenses. Without the demarcation between work and home that a physical office provides, it can be easy to slip into the habit of just paying for work-related expenses yourself. A few sticky notes here, some folders for presentations there, your work-related Wi-Fi… the costs can add up.

If these expenses are genuinely for work they should be treated that way. If you are an employee and entitled to claim these costs back: claim them. You don't need to pay for these things out of a sense of being grateful to be allowed to work from home. If you are a consultant or have your own business include your costs in your fee structure. At the very least include them as expenses in your business accounts.

Find out what you are able to claim – ask your manager or talk to your accountant or financial advisor to make sure that you are getting back what you are entitled to. Looking after yourself financially is important to your peace of mind and well-being.

95. Drink water

A study by the Universities of East London and Westminster in the UK found that people who were thirsty and drank water had an improved speed of responding on task performance.[x] *(Another reason is the need to, you know, stay alive!)*

I always admire the people who are super organized and have a jug of water conveniently placed on their desk ready to keep hydrated all day – no excuse for them not to keep working and have ready access to the good stuff. Personally, I worry about knocking the jug over and ending up with a floating keyboard and soggy papers.

On the bright side I have found those trips to the kitchen to refill my glass are not only a chance to replenish my water supply, but also a good chance to get moving. While the 62-step round-trip from my office to the kitchen sink does not add much to my daily tally it does get me out of my chair. It also makes me take a short break from whatever I am working on. And, because I am easily distracted, it can often lead to a slightly longer break than planned, a bit more walking, and time to actually think about what I am working on.

There are plenty of other ways to make sure you are getting enough H_2O:

- Drink a glass while you are waiting for the kettle to boil or the coffee to brew.

- Fill your glass or bottle as soon as it is empty.

- Refill your glass every time you take a bathroom break *(this will, of course, be a cyclical process)*.

- Mark a water bottle so you can keep track of how much you have drunk.

- Get a little bit glamorous with sparkling or mineral water, or add some fresh fruit.

- Set an alarm to remind yourself *(and if you get confused and think it's time for a break or a walk that's good too!).*

- Drink a glass before every meal.

- Invest in a water filter to improve the taste.

- Try the jug of water on your desk trick. *(I am sure not everyone is as clumsy as me... or get one with a lid!)*

There are even apps to help monitor how much water you are drinking. *(Of course there are!)*

Feeling thirsty now? Go on, grab a glass of water!

96. Have healthy snacks on hand

A number of people I speak to mention the pantry and refrigerator as danger zones when they work from home. Locks are often proposed as the possible solution *(possibly only effective if you throw away the key?)* An alternative to making your access to snacks as difficult as possible is to have healthy ones in easy reach.

It's easy to find yourself standing with the refrigerator door open, staring in, and looking for a tempting treat. You probably wouldn't do it in the office kitchen *(well you might),* but it's more likely when you work from home and you're only a short distance from both the kitchen and temptation.

When you are at home, your options for snacks will be whatever you, or someone you live with, buy. So having healthy options available requires a little bit of planning, and shopping, to make sure they are there when you need them.

Consider stocking up the cupboard or refrigerator with some of these snacks:

- Nuts
- Fruit
- Rice cakes and avocado, nut butters and healthy spreads
- Roasted chickpeas
- Edamame
- Yogurt (unsweetened)
- Hummus with celery or carrot sticks *(you can cheat and buy these pre-cut)*
- Protein bars
- Trail mix

- Pumpkin or sunflower seeds

- Roasted seaweed

- Dark chocolate, and

- Wasabi peas.

The one thing these snacks have in common? They need no preparation! If you have a few minutes and a little inspiration, there are no doubt hundreds of tasty, healthy morsels that you can whip up to look after yourself. Whether you opt for gourmet creations or pre-packaged healthy snacks, your waistline, energy levels and productivity are all likely winners. And you can enjoy feeling a little bit virtuous, too!

97. Buy a fish

My niece Lily once asked me, *"Auntie Karen, are you a dog person or a cat person?"* Her younger sister, Bella, without giving me a chance to even think how to explain that I have trouble keeping plants alive let alone animals, immediately responded, *"She is a dog person, of course!"* Needless to say Bella is a dog person.

Regardless of your choice of animal friend there is no doubt that their owners *(a term used loosely for cat custodians as the master/servant relationship is a bit ambiguous)* revel in the extra time that working from home provides to spend with their pet.

Despite cats on keyboards, dogs barking, and birds chirping during phone calls there are a lot of upsides to having a pet. They are frequently the subject of social media posts extolling the virtues of working from home.

Pets provide companionship, a good excuse for a walk *(with a dog or to look for a cat)*, and they are great listeners. I'm not sure if they will sit still long enough for a full presentation rehearsal and they are unlikely to give you feedback, but at least you don't feel stupid when you ask them a question out loud, as you do, when there is no human being in close proximity.

Fish are not quite as responsive or cuddly as other pets *(to say the least)*, but an aquarium can be quite calming and pretty to look at. There is no rule that says you can't talk to them as well and feeding them every day is a good reason to stand up and have a short break from work.

Seriously though, one of the downsides of working from home is the potential to feel isolated. A pet is a great companion, and one of the joys of working from home for many people. If you are a pet owner, even if you don't work at home full time, there is a fair chance that both you and Fido are going to enjoy the days when you do.

This is not a replacement for interactions with actual human beings but an option to consider for some companionship throughout the day.

As for me, I have now made the commitment to a terrarium *(well actually a choice that was made for me – thanks Sandy)*, so I'll see how I go keeping it alive before I take on any further responsibilities. I'll work my way up to buying a fish.

98. Take vacations

There are many, many excellent reasons to take your vacations: plane food, crowded tourist sites, security screening, slimy sunscreen… *(Hang on this is the wrong list but even they may not discourage you!)*

Among the many wonderful reasons to take your vacations are: time for yourself and your family; the chance to wind down, relax and re-energize; the opportunity to see or learn something new; plus it's good for your health, creativity and, ultimately, your productivity when you return to work. Not to mention they can be just plain fun.

There's plenty of research that supports that vacations are beneficial. These include internal research by EY (the old Ernst & Young) that showed that for every 10 hours of vacation time their US and Canadian staff took, their average performance-review results were 8% higher.[xi] There is a raft of other studies that link vacations with improvements in life satisfaction and mental health, reduced risk of heart disease, and improved productivity.[xii]

A study that was conducted over nine years by the University of New York found that for people who took a vacation every year, the risk of death was reduced by up to 30% due to heart disease and overall by 20%.[xiii] Another study, this one over a 20-year period, of women who participated in the Framingham Heart Study found that women were about eight times more likely to have a heart attack or develop heart disease if they had a vacation only every six years (or less) compared to women who took at least two vacations a year.[xiv] This is serious, folks! Vacations can be the difference between life and death!

But not everybody takes them. Research by software company, Kimble Applications found that 47% of Americans didn't take their vacation time in 2017, and 21% "left more than five vacation days on the table."[xv] What a waste!

People have a variety reasons for not taking time off. Common justifications include having too much work to do; nobody to do the work while they are away; and a fear of the boss realizing that they could be replaced or that their temporary fill is doing a better job than they do.

When you work for yourself it can be even harder to take a break and it often means no pay. This requires planning ahead and building the time off into your financial plan.

Don't fall into the trap of thinking that just because you work in your own environment that you don't need a break from your job. Sure you may not need a break from the office environment, but what about a break from emails, customers, your boss, and the general pressures of work. If you work from home you *are* working and all the usual, very good reasons for taking a vacation still apply.

Take your vacations, look after and enjoy yourself. You deserve and need them. Have some fun!

99. Enjoy the flexibility

One of the big, big benefits of working from home is the flexibility. The trick is to remember to use it – not to fall into the trap of cooping yourself up in your home office, hour after hour, and not taking advantage of the many options you could be weaving into *(and enjoying during)* your day.

There's also a good chance that the time you take away from your desk is only going to increase your productivity. Microsoft in Japan recently trialled a four-day working week and had a 40% improvement in productivity and their employees were happier.[xvi] Provided you do what you need to do, there is no need to feel guilty about managing your time in a way that works for you because you are likely to be just as, if not more, productive.

There are swings and roundabouts, as they say, and there are, no doubt, many occasions when you need to be flexible to fit in with work. When you can, manage your time and make your work fit in with you.

Rejoice and enjoy the flexibility that you have to potentially:

- Schedule appointments during the day.
- Multi-task and get some chores done.
- Go for a walk.
- Be home for deliveries.
- Juggle your family responsibilities.
- Enjoy time with your pooch or kitty.
- Bake a cake.
- Start early.
- Exercise before work.

- Take 10 minutes extra to enjoy your coffee.
- Finish late.
- Sleep in.
- Dress comfortably.
- Go to the gym in the middle of the day.
- Finish early.
- Sneak in some TV time while the house is quiet.
- Start late.
- Treat yourself to some pampering.
- Pick up the kids from school.
- Read a chapter in a book.
- Prepare dinner in the middle of the day.
- Work in your pajamas.

And so on! I suspect that I have barely scratched the surface of the practical and/or enjoyable activities that you could be incorporating into your days. Not to mention 'investing' the time and money you would have spent commuting in yourself *(just an extra little idea you might want to pick up and run with!)*.

Enjoying your flexibility, guilt-free, is fundamental to making the very most of working from home and looking after yourself.

AND FINALLY,

100. Own it!

Bec Bell is an executive with a large corporation and business owner who lives in a regional area in Australia. When I asked for her number-one tip for working from home, Bec said, *"Embrace it! Don't try and pretend you are in an office – you're not!"* She also recommends letting people know that you work from home. *"Be proud, don't shy away from it,"* she advised. This really resonated with me.

I've also found it easier to tell people that I regularly talk to that I work from home. Sure, some people just don't need to know where you are or how you are working; their only concern is if you get the work done for them that you need to do. But when its people you regularly speak with it can help skip over interruptions *(think barking dog, squawking birds or people in the background)* if they know you are not in an office. If your regular contacts know that you are at home, a quick *"Oh, that's just the dog"* when Fido decides to make his presence felt helps you quickly explain the distraction and keep going with your call. Even though you may put the phone on mute and be dealing with the aforementioned Fido at the same time!

Be proud of your decision to work from home. It is a legitimate work and lifestyle choice. It may be a necessity rather than a choice because as a business owner or contractor you don't want to incur the cost of renting an office *(one of the best tips I was given)* or you are remote from your employer and commuting isn't an option. Whatever the reason, it's not a perk or a disadvantage. It's just the way you work.

If anyone thinks that you have it too easy or are not pulling your weight *(provided it's not your manager or your client)*, that's their problem. You know the reality of starting early, finishing late and the extra effort you need to make to stay connected. They don't need to know and you don't have to tell them. You shouldn't feel the need to apologize or explain to anyone else.

The other aspect of 'owning' working from home is to take advantage of all the good stuff. Start late, finish early, arrange your day for personal commitments, work in your pajamas *(gasp)*, whatever works for you! And whatever you do… don't feel guilty about it.

The secret is to embrace the freedom and the opportunities, and manage the downsides. Make it work for you. Own it!

101. The pajamas dilemma

The big question is, can you be Professional in Pajamas? The late-night call, the early-morning start to nail a presentation in peace and quiet before the phone starts ringing, the day's calls and meetings starting early and you not getting a break... these are just some of the many reasons why working in pajamas can be part of the reality of working from home. But can you do your best work?

To resolve this question I took a very scientific approach and turned to the people of Twitter and Facebook for their opinion. Opinion was divided *(completely shocking that this would ever happen on social media!).*

In my Facebook poll, 92.2 % of people who participated said that they work from home, and 57% said that they thought, yes, you could be professional in pajamas. Another 13% didn't give a full thumbs up to the concept but thought that there were some circumstances when it was okay. So let's count that as 70% as reasonably in favor.

Some qualified their responses: *"Absolutely, but only when not on a video conference"*; *"Depends on the individual"*; and *"Depends on what I am doing."* One person explained their reluctance: *"I need to feel clean, organized and ready to start the day! Having said that, if I'm working at night I might be in my pajamas, but it's not often."*

The folks on Twitter were slightly more supportive of working in pajamas with 75% of votes positive and another 6% choosing the option 'Maybe (if it's cold)'. *(Like I said the poll was very scientific!)*

There are certainly people on Twitter who are proud to declare that they work in their sleepwear. Home entrepreneur and YouTuber @bloggingrapper tweeted a picture of his Mutant Ninja Turtle pajamas with the hashtags #workfromhome #pajamas; Graphic Designer @aunimilne confessed: *"The truth is if I didn't have to walk my dogs every day it's possible I would never get out of my pajamas."* Illustrator @kovahs_art declared: *"Being a freelancer means having a pair of work pajamas. Mine are Christmas red cookie monster ones. I wear them all year round..."* Although there was a warning from @mayapankalla

"Never assume a 9am conference call with a new client is not a video call." I can only imagine what led to that tweet!

There are many of us who do work in our pajamas. HRnews reported a study of 1000 people in the UK who work from home: 28% of people said that they sometimes work in their pajamas.[i] As a sample of one, I must confess that I am very partial to an early start in the morning in pajamas and then a break for a shower, coffee and some more formal clothes *(shorts or jeans depending on the season)*.

I do agree with musician @jourdanhines who tweeted *"It's a good day when the wardrobe change goes from #pajamas to #yogaPants and back to pajamas."* I'm a bit more inclined to activewear myself, but the sentiment is the same. I don't work any less hard, I don't work any less effectively, and I certainly don't work any less professionally.

One of the responses on my Facebook poll to 'Can you be professional in pajamas?' was *"If you are professional to begin with then, yes, but if you are not professional (which includes being diligent) then, no."* I'd go a step further and say for those who are not able to be professional regardless of what they are wearing; working from home is unlikely to be a very successful gig for them.

There are plenty of experts out there who advise getting dressed as the ideal start to a productive day. For some people, that is completely correct. However, many others can work efficiently and productively regardless of where they are or what they wear. It needs to be right for you.

Can you be professional in pajamas? It's your choice.

And that's why working from home is so good!

Stay in Touch

I have set up a couple of groups on social media - so that we connect, collaborate, and share even more tips with each other:

On Facebook – Professional in Pajamas: 101 Tips for Working from Home

On LinkedIn – Professional in Pajamas: Tips for Working from Home

I thought I better give them slight different names or I'd get too confused! Alternatively you can keep in touch with me at:

Careertipstogo.com where I blog.

On LinkedIn - linkedin.com/in/karenadamedes

Or on Twitter - @karenadamedes

If you've found **Professional in Pajamas: 101 Tips for Working from Home** helpful, insightful or awesome *(or all of the above!)*, I would really appreciate it if you could leave a review wherever you bought it online.

Look forward to connecting with you!

Karen Adamedes

About the Author

Karen Adamedes specializes in business transformation for organizations as a **strategic business adviser,** and career transformation as an **author, blogger, and speaker.** Karen lives just outside of Sydney in Australia, with her husband and a terrarium of plants that she is desperately trying to keep alive.

The allure of figuring out 'how things work' for organizations, processes, and people *(as opposed to anything that involves a screwdriver or a wrench)*, and how they could work better led Karen into the world of business and career transformation.

Karen has worked from home for the last decade, both as a senior executive and as a consultant to organizations in many industries, including IT, Health, and Insurance, as well as the Not for Profit sector. From the comfort of her home she has successfully negotiated multi-million dollar deals, led national teams, and delivered major projects *(and written this book!)*.

Her career insights have been featured on the pages of major magazines and newspapers, appeared regularly in international publications, and in her first book, **Hot Tips for Career Chicks: Unlocking the CODE to Success.** Karen's blog careertipstogo.com has been included in the Top 100 Career Blogs on Feedspot and ThriveYard.

Karen's extensive working-from-home experience – both the things that work and those that are a little bit tricky – led her to write her second book, **Professional in Pajamas: 101 Tips for Working from Home**.

While she's never been tempted to mow the lawn while working from home, she admits that she does sometimes work in her pajamas!

Endnotes

WORK FROM HOME

[i] https://www.nytimes.com/2017/02/15/us/remote-workers-work-from-home.html

[ii] https://www.abs.gov.au/ausstats/abs@.nsf/mediareleasesbyCatalogue/630DCF813FED0E0CCA258113001878F2?OpenDocument

[iii] https://www.bbc.com/news/business-27694938

[iv] https://www.cbc.ca/news/business/telecommuting-growing-as-companies-look-to-save-money-respond-to-employees-1.3596420

[v] https://www.irishtimes.com/life-and-style/homes-and-property/the-bearable-commute-time-is-45-minutes-new-study-finds-1.3704401

[vi] https://www.eurofound.europa.eu/publications/report/2017/working-anytime-anywhere-the-effects-on-the-world-of-work

[vii] https://qz.com/765908/flexible-working-is-making-us-work-longer/

[viii] https://journals.sagepub.com/doi/10.1177/0018726709349199

[ix] https://www.inc.com/bill-murphy-jr/people-who-work-from-home-are-happier-more-efficient-according-to-this-fascinating-study-theres-only-1-catch.html

I GETTING STUFF DONE

[i] https://medium.com/thrive-global/this-simple-method-can-help-you-figure-out-your-most-productive-time-of-day-378c077fd67d

[ii] https://www.businessinsider.com.au/10-minute-trick-to-boost-your-productivity-2016-1?r=US&IR=T

[iii] https://medium.com/the-mission/the-science-backed-ways-music-affects-your-brain-and-productivity-e11145079305

[iv] https://www.cbsnews.com/news/do-you-check-your-phone-more-than-most-americans/

[v] https://www.huffingtonpost.co.uk/entry/brits-now-check-their-mobile-phones-every-12-minutes_uk_5b62bf60e4b0b15aba9fe3cb?guce_referrer_us=aHR0cHM6Ly93d3cuZ29vZ2xlLmNvbS8&guce_referrer_cs=6BqD0I7JuUnz0LNFidEcMw&_guc_consent_skip=1586921956

[vi] https://www.lifewire.com/how-many-emails-are-sent-every-day-1171210

[vii] https://onlinelibrary.wiley.com/doi/abs/10.1111/j.1468-005X.2011.00272.x

[viii] https://www.rdasia.com/true-stories-lifestyle/work/The-Benefits-of-Taking-Breaks

[ix] https://www.psychologytoday.com/us/blog/changepower/201704/how-do-work-breaks-help-your-brain-5-surprising-answers

[x] https://www.nytimes.com/2012/06/17/jobs/take-breaks-regularly-to-stay-on-schedule-workstation.html

[xi] https://francescocirillo.com/pages/pomodoro-technique

[xii] https://www.themuse.com/advice/the-rule-of-52-and-17-its-random-but-it-ups-your-productivity

[xiii] https://www.cdc.gov/family/minutes/tips/takeabreak/index.htm

[xiv] https://www.monash.edu/about/editorialstyle/planning/define-your-goals

II WORK VERSUS HOME

[i] https://www.eurofound.europa.eu/publications/report/2017/working-anytime-anywhere-the-effects-on-the-world-of-work

[ii] https://www.hbs.edu/faculty/Pages/item.aspx?num=52953

[iii] https://www.bloomberg.com/news/videos/2017-01-30/bill-gates-and-warren-buffett-charlie-rose

iv https://www.eurofound.europa.eu/publications/report/2017/working-anytime-anywhere-the-effects-on-the-world-of-work

III   WHERE YOU WORK

i https://www.psychologytoday.com/au/blog/the-athletes-way/201306/exposure-natural-light-improves-workplace-performance

ii https://www.ccohs.ca/oshanswers/ergonomics/lighting_survey.html

iii https://indoor.lbl.gov/sites/all/files/lbnl-60946.pdf

iv https://www.businessnewsdaily.com/10964-office-temperature-debate.html

v https://www.ergotron.com/en-au/ergonomics/ergonomic-equation

IV   TECHNOLOGY

i https://medium.com/@mfornasa/remote-working-is-your-internet-connection-good-enough-7e5c8d4f59b2

ii https://www.maketecheasier.com/do-dual-monitors-improve-productivity/

V   CONFERENCING

i https://qz.com/703513/too-many-workers-arent-wearing-pants-on-video-calls/

ii https://www.westuc.com/files/InterCall-Mobile_Conferencing-FINAL.jpg

VII   CAREER DEVELOPMENT

i https://www.theguardian.com/education/2015/mar/09/adult-education-funding-cuts-lifelong-learning-investment

VIII WELL-BEING

i https://annals.org/aim/article-abstract/2653704/patterns-sedentary-behavior-mortality-u-s-middle-aged-older-adults

ii https://www.npr.org/sections/health-shots/2015/05/01/403523463/two-minutes-of-walking-an-hour-boosts-health-but-its-no-panacea

iii https://www.eurofound.europa.eu/publications/report/2017/working-anytime-anywhere-the-effects-on-the-world-of-work

iv https://www.weforum.org/agenda/2019/03/flexible-working-can-make-work-life-worse-germany/

v https://qz.com/765908/flexible-working-is-making-us-work-longer/

vi https://www.ahajournals.org/doi/10.1161/STROKEAHA.119.025454

vii https://open.buffer.com/state-remote-work-2018/#benefits

viii https://rlc.randstadusa.com/press-room/press-releases/randstad-us-and-apartment-guide-survey-reveals-how-rising-living-expenses-impact-americans-work-and-housing-decisions-1

ix https://www.nytimes.com/2017/02/15/us/remote-workers-work-from-home.html

x https://www.frontiersin.org/articles/10.3389/fnhum.2013.00363/full

xi https://www.cnbc.com/2014/08/27/vacations-help-you-get-ahead-at-work-ey.html

xii https://www.apadivisions.org/division-28/publications/newsletters/psychopharmacology/2017/07/vacation

xiii http://www.clevelandheartlab.com/blog/vacations-and-your-heart/

xiv http://www.clevelandheartlab.com/blog/vacations-and-your-heart/

xv https://www.forbes.com/sites/victorlipman/2018/05/21/why-america-has-become-the-no-vacation-nation/#6c9230424c53

xvi https://www.theguardian.com/technology/2019/nov/04/microsoft-japan-four-day-work-week-productivity

AND FINALLY

i http://hrnews.co.uk/national-pyjama-week-28-of-uk-employees-who-work-from-home-do-so-in-their-pyjamas/

www.ingramcontent.com/pod-product-compliance
Lightning Source LLC
Chambersburg PA
CBHW050633300426
44112CB00012B/1775